A FOREST OF PENCILS

A FOREST OF PENCILS

*The Story of Schools
Through the Ages*

by

WINIFRED TRASK LEE

illustrated by Heidi Palmer

THE BOBBS-MERRILL COMPANY, INC.
Indianapolis   New York

The Bobbs-Merrill Company, Inc.
Publishers Indianapolis New York
Text copyright © 1973 by Winifred Trask Lee
Illustrations copyright © 1973 by Heidi Palmer
Design by Jack Jaget
Printed in the United States of America
ISBN: 0–672–51781–7
Library of Congress catalog card number: 73–1751
0 9 8 7 6 5 4 3 2 1

For
WINIFRED TRASK GORDON
with my love

Contents

CONTENTS

EARLY MODERN

Foreword

"Bo-Do did not have to read his book. He had no book to read."

Not long ago this enviable cave boy, with his matted hair and weapons of flint, was the hero of countless households of children. His life, as depicted in a favorite first reader, was enticing. He could grapple with wild beasts; he struck fire from stones. He went naked, and never had to wash his hands. He could choose his own bedtime, curling up on a bearskin in a corner of the family cave when weariness interrupted his delightful pursuits. Best of all, he did not have to go to school.

What destroyed that idyllic ignorance of the cave boy? How did civilization, with its rules and schools and responsibilities, overtake the descendants of Bo-Do?

Since the cave man could not write, we of course have no exact records of his progress from barbarism. But from studies of later primitive peoples, we can figure out a general pattern.

Long before there were schools, there was teaching. Even

the most primitive parents passed along to their children such knowledge as they had. Had they not done so, each generation would have had to discover for itself how to make fire or scratch a message.

Successive generations made new discoveries—how to make better implements, and how to use the sun and wind and rain to their advantage. They learned how to make marks with sharpened tools to express a meaning—an arrow to point out a direction, or a crude drawing of an animal to show where game

had been sighted. They watched the skies and speculated on their changes; and what they thus learned about space and time and the passing of seasons, they taught to their children.

They taught them, too, the difference between good and evil: which actions were for the good of the tribe, and which would arouse its anger. Like all parents, they wanted their children to survive. And if their young people did not behave in ways acceptable to the tribe, they were cast out and left to the mercy of wild animals.

Primitive men revered the elemental forces, which to them were gods. They taught their children the same religious reverence. They also taught them to honor their heroes: perhaps a man who had served the tribe well by finding meat in time of famine; or one who could draw an effective picture; or one who had found berries and plant juices for staining clay with bright colors; or one who had led them to victory over warring neighbors; or one who had visions beyond the daily round of killing and eating and sleeping, and whose words brought hope and wonder to the tribe.

We do not know at what point in prehistory a "wise man" was chosen to teach the tribe's children. But we may be sure that when this came about, early man encouraged his sons to listen to the words of wisdom. And we may be equally sure that when his young son became cleverer than he, the father was more proud of him than of any accomplishments of his own.

Thus, with knowledge accumulating through thousands of generations, came civilization.

Not, of course, that knowledge flowed from ancient to modern times in one ever-widening stream. Rather, like underground currents, it sprang to light in different parts of the earth, among different tribes and nations. As these various peoples came in contact with one another, through either conquest or peaceful exploration, they picked up one another's knowledge and added it to their own. At certain points in history, such connected sources of knowledge surged into a wide wave of enlightenment, spreading over surrounding countries. Sometimes, too, such a wave would carry some rather unfortunate flotsam of misinformation, such as various superstitions and the "science" of magic. But on the whole, knowledge proved useful to man, easing his toil and uplifting his heart.

As the bulk of human knowledge increased in various lands, it became too vast for an ordinary man to master, let alone to teach to his children. Specialists arose—scribes who could read and write, scholars who could decipher other tongues and understand other ways of thinking. And, since men of learning are usually pleased to pass along the fruits of their studies, there arose schools.

What were they like, those early schools?

"School," said a small boy, "is where you go and sit in a row when you are six."

He took it quite for granted—schools are there, and children must attend them. He had no idea how recent this law was. Ancient schools were few, and they were certainly not overcrowded. Schooling was a luxury available only to those children who were considered bright enough to be worthy of it, whose parents could afford it, and who lived near enough to a school to be able to walk to it. For many, many centuries, only a few boys in any given town—and even fewer girls—were privileged to go to school at all.

But as the world's knowledge increased, so did the number of schools and scholars. They were very different from our schools of today. Moreover, like language and styles of dress, they varied in time and place. Each taught what was considered important at the time; each used such materials as were at hand for writing and counting. Each, no doubt, did its best to improve the minds and lives of its young scholars.

It may interest young people of today to look at some of those schools of other times and other places.

ANCIENT
TIMES

China

What heaven has conferred is called nature; an accordance with nature is called the path of duty; the regulation of this path is called instruction.

—CONFUCIUS

Some three thousand years ago, a Chinese boy arose at cockcrow and got ready for school. He dressed with great care, putting on his clothes in the special and exact order that he had been taught was most pleasing to the gods.

Bear in mind that this was more than a thousand years before the birth of Christ. Aryan tribes still roamed the lands that are now Europe, tending their flocks and learning to use iron. England was inhabited by quarrelsome families of Celts living in rude huts and, for knowledge, looking to priests who painted their faces blue and practiced human sacrifice. As for America, its existence was unknown to anyone except its native Indians —who doubtless believed it to be the whole world.

But the far, golden land of China was already old in culture. It was a land of palaces and gongs, of princes and poets, of silks and music and beautiful objects made of jade or clay or bronze. And it was a country where learning was revered above all.

In China, scholars were held in higher esteem than princes. They advised the emperor and the nobles on how to rule the provinces that made up the loosely knit empire. Scholars knew best how to please the gods and how to deal justly with the people. For they, and only they, could read the intricate picture writing, which set down the rules and rituals of wisdom.

As the empire grew, more men of learning were needed to serve the government. So the Emperor Wu Wang, in 1122 B.C., ordered schools built in his capital, where boys might start their training to become government officials. It was said that any clever boy was welcome at these schools—the son of a poor fisherman along with the sons of the emperor. The nobles under Wu Wang followed his example and set up schools in their own provinces, so that soon there were schools throughout China. These, it is believed, were the first organized schools in the world.

Our Chinese schoolboy, as we have said, dressed himself according to ritual. First he washed his hands and rinsed his mouth. Next he combed his hair, covered it with a piece of silk, attached the silk with a hairpin, bound it with a fillet, smoothed it, and put on his cap. Having finished with his head, he put on his jacket and knee covers, buckled his girdle around his waist, and tucked his wooden writing tablet in front. The tools he would need for the day he hung from his girdle: on the left side, his knife and whetstone, his handkerchief and duster, a small spike for boring holes, and his metal speculum for getting fire from the sun; on the right side, the leather thumb cover and armlet he used for archery, and a cylinder containing his writing tools. Thus decked out, he put on his leggings and shoes and tied his laces.

His next duty was to attend his elders. The fact that he was the young scholar of the family did not excuse him from the Chinese custom of serving his parents and grandparents and any other relatives who might be living in the house. He went to their rooms and bowed; he asked after their health and their needs. If they fancied some breakfast at that hour, he prepared and carried it to them before eating his own. He was careful to be neat in the kitchen so as not to annoy his friend Chang Kung, the kitchen god, whose portrait hung above the stove and who brought him good things on feast days.

His chores finished, he left the house, saluting the household gods as he went. He bowed to the god of the door, the god of the court, the god of the path, and the god of the gate. Then, through the dawn, he set out to walk to the house of the scholar-teacher who would guide his young brain along the difficult path to wisdom.

The schoolroom was clamorous with voices, their shrill chant spilling out into the street. For the Chinese school was what is called a "loud school"; the teacher would recite a phrase and the pupils would repeat it after him, each chanting it aloud to fix it in his mind. Learning had to be by repetition since there were few books to be had for study. In fact, there were no books as we know them—for this was long before printing was invented. Chinese books were handwritten in delicate Chinese characters on thin strips of bamboo or wood fastened together with a leather thong to form a "volume." So rare were these volumes that the teacher carried their contents in his head, having committed them to memory. Small wonder that a teacher was respected! To be worthy of the name of scholar, he had to know several hundred volumes by heart.

Seated on a thin mat on the floor, repeating his master's words phrase by phrase, the schoolboy learned his lessons.

They were quite different from the lessons of today. He learned little arithmetic or science, since very little was known of those matters. Not much history, because almost nothing was known about the rest of the world, and even China's own history was largely made up of legends and hearsay. His lessons

were all contained in a body of rules called "Right Behavior," for to be perfect in oneself was considered the chief object of wisdom. And to achieve such perfection one must live in a carefully balanced harmony with all things—with one's fellows, with nature, with the sun and the moon and the seasons. This harmony, it was believed, could be attained only by carrying out the many, many rules that had been laid down by generations of wise men.

The first rules for a schoolboy to learn were called the "Five Relationships." These concerned the proper behavior between parent and child, husband and wife, ruler and subjects, older and younger brothers, and friend and friend. As soon as he was letter-perfect in these rules, the boy went on to the "Five Virtues": kindness, good manners, knowledge, uprightness, and honor. All these qualities, the Chinese felt, were as natural to man as his hands or his eyes; the rules were to help develop them properly.

Reading and writing—the subjects that we think of today as the start of all lessons—were more difficult for the Chinese boy. To begin with, there were no letters. Although the Chinese were among the first people to use "writing," they had no alphabet. They began to write, as will any bright child, by making a picture of the word they wished to express. Those pictures became symbols. The symbol ⊙ meant the *sun.* △△△ stood for *mountains. River* was 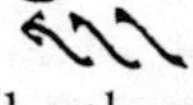 ; *child* was  . Since each noun had to be pictured rather than spelled, there were, of course, hundreds of such *pictographs* to be learned. Then there were all the words that could not be pictured but had to be expressed somehow, requiring hundreds more signs. The symbol  , indicating a river that was blocked, stood for *misfortune.* A symbol that depicted a woman with a child meant *good;* and the symbol for *home* was a woman under a roof. Such compound picture signs are called ideograms. A third kind of symbol, called a phonogram, expressed only the *sound* of the word—as if, in English, we were to write the verb *see* by using a picture of the sea.

At first, these symbols for words had been carefully drawn with a sharp metal tool. But when scholars started using brushes dipped in ink for faster writing, the symbols changed into forms more easily made by the strokes of a brush. ⊙ for *sun* became 玉 ; *mountain* became 𝚼𝚼𝚼 ; *child* became 𝒥 . *Mouth*, ○ , became a square 口 ; and if it spouted lines like this, 言 , it meant *words*.

In order to learn how to write, then, the Chinese boy had to master the eight basic strokes of the brush, then the word symbols. Since there were some 80,000 of these, it is doubtful if many boys learned them all.

Reading was even more complicated than writing. Chinese characters, then as now, were written in vertical rows, to be read from top to bottom and from right to left—not in itself a difficulty if one had been taught to read that way. But the characters, having no spelling, had no exact sounds; they were pictures of ideas, so that to read them was like translating ideas into language. The symbol 上 , for instance, can mean *above* or *top man* and can be used to indicate a ruler such as a king or chief. But it can also mean *best* or *on top of*; or it may mean either the verb *to mount* or the verb *to go to*. It is easy to see that characters having so many possible meanings could be read as sentences having no meaning at all. The art of reading, therefore, was to interpret the characters into language that was both meaningful and strong.

There were other subjects, too, to break the monotony of reading and writing and learning by rote. The boys learned to play lutes, flutes, and bells, making the sliding, watery music that seems so exotic to our Western ears. They worked at archery, too, and horsemanship. Older boys might compete in chariot races. The chariots were crude, their iron wheels making a rough ride. But to Chinese youths such races were a kingly sport.

The school day lasted from dawn to dusk. Discipline was strict: boys who did not attend to their work were severely beaten. If a boy's hand got into mischief, he was made to hold it palm upward over the edge of a table to receive a sharp and agonizing whack. For carelessness in writing or blots on his wooden tablet, his punishment was to drink a dish of ink. The ink, made of lampblack, gum, and water, was not poisonous—but it was certainly not tasty. And if, after all the teacher's efforts, the boy continued to be lazy or careless, he was sent to a neighboring province in the hope that a change of scene would mend his habits. If this did not cure him, he was simply exiled to a "barbarous land"—a great relief, no doubt, to his parents and teacher.

No girls attended these schools. It was many hundreds of years before girls were sent to school—in this or any other land. And only a small percentage of boys had this privilege. The teacher-scholar required a fee, however small; and the great masses of Chinese people were without money. Besides, peasant folk needed their sons at home to help with the plowing and planting, the fishing and the cutting of wood.

But if a boy seemed extremely bright, the whole family made a great effort to send him to school. (Chinese families were large and closely knit, and relatives contributed what they could.) For was not this his great opportunity to become a man of learning, an official of government? As for his farm chores, there is an ancient Chinese drawing of a praiseworthy lad driving an ox-drawn plow, his book strapped to the horns of the ox so that he may study his lesson while plowing.

So the Chinese schools went on as best they could, teaching the word-of-mouth "rules" and reading and writing, until 551 B.C., when there appeared the great teacher Confucius—or Kung Fu-tsu in the Chinese tongue. This gentle scholar, whose sayings are still quoted today, was willing to teach whoever came to him in return for whatever they could afford—even a dried fish or a portion of rice. His teachings and ideas were spread by his pupils throughout the land. Somehow, with all his work, he found time to gather all Chinese books into an ordered series of wooden volumes that became the Chinese "Classics." This series included books of history, philosophy, poetry, and rites and ceremonies, along with volumes of Confucius's own commentaries. The Classics, carefully copied by scholars, became the standard textbooks of Chinese schools.

In the third century B.C. the Classics were nearly lost to the world. The emperor Shi Huang Ti, who built the Great Wall of China, became angry with the scholars for criticizing his warlike character. To punish them he ordered all books to be destroyed—except for a few on farming and magic, which he considered really useful subjects. The scholars refused to hand over their precious books, hiding them in their homes. Outraged, Shi Huang Ti ordered his soldiers to seize both books and scholars. The books he burned; and the scholars, some four hundred of them, he buried alive in the Great Wall. But one set of books, so the story goes, was successfully hidden by the grandson of Confucius. Another generation of scholars patiently copied them, and the Classics again became the basis of Chinese schools.

As learning spread, competition for government jobs became stronger. During the Han dynasty (about 200 B.C.) the government set up its famous and fearsome system of examinations for sifting its would-be scholars.

"First examinations" were held every three years in each district. They were open to boys who had finished school and who therefore could read, write, and repeat a dozen or so books by heart. The examination went on for twenty-four hours, with the youths sitting in separate cells, like isolated prisoners, while grappling with their tasks. They were given three quotations on which to write essays—two from the Classics and one from the "book of poetry." The Classics themes were puzzlers such as: "To possess ability, and yet ask of those who do not; to know much, and yet inquire of those who know little; to possess, and yet to appear not to possess; to be full, and yet to appear empty"; or, "He took hold of things by their two extremes, and in his dealings with the people maintained the golden medium." The student was expected to adorn his essays with plenty of quotations from the old scholars; but the wording must be his own, and in beautiful language. Then, from a poetic phrase such as: "The sound of the oar and the green of the hill and the water," he had to compose an exquisite prose poem.

The standard of these essays was very high. Only one out of twenty students passed the examination. And woe betide an aspiring scholar who tried to smuggle notes into his cell! He was expelled immediately, never again to be allowed to take the tests. Youths who did pass, however, were given the title of "flower of talent" and were now eligible for minor positions in government.

"Second examinations" were held every few years at the capital of the province. The "flowers" would journey there for an ordeal that, this time, was to last three days. Each day they would be given three classical themes about which to write. In addition, they had to compose original essays on some timely subject, such as justice or taxes, that was of importance to the whole nation. This time, only one student in a hundred passed. Those who did so were entitled "promoted scholars."

The promoted scholar was an important person. He could wear a special button on his cap and hang a sign above his door proclaiming him a literary man. And he was now eligible for a high official position.

"Third examinations," the highest, were for those whose lives were truly devoted to scholarship. They were held from time to time at the imperial capital, where the contestants, youths no longer but men who had spent years in study, would travel. Of these, the six best were rewarded with a passing mark. But that reward was great; they were now members of the Imperial Board of Education—or, as the Chinese delightfully called it, the Forest of Pencils. And to belong to the Forest of Pencils was the highest honor to be had in China.

The Near East

The very ancient civilizations of the Near East—the Sumerians, Babylonians, Assyrians and Chaldeans, and the Egyptians of the Nile valley—all had schools of sorts. But their schools were fewer and more limited than those of China. They might almost be called vocational schools, for they trained boys to become scribes, men who could write.

All groups of people, early in their cultures, have found the need to communicate by writing. They have done this by means of pictures; or by symbols, representing words or ideas or simple syllables; or, finally, by marks for sounds, like the letters of our own alphabet. Before the use of such letters, the scribes of the various peoples managed to write by means of several ingenious methods, using such writing materials as came to hand.

The *Sumerians* wrote on clay. They flattened the wet clay to a tile and made thin triangular marks on it with the sharp corner of a cut reed, creating the writing known as cuneiform. Groups of these wedge-shaped marks formed symbols for words that had been originally pictured, such as 㠪 for ⌐ (*foot*). It is often very difficult to trace the original picture from the cuneiform writing. However, the marks made patterns that were quite beautiful, rather like the prints made by shore birds on a wet beach. To our eyes, they are intricate and mysterious.

They were mysterious, too, to most Sumerians. For the art of writing, half sacred and half magic, was limited to priests and their scribes. They alone could translate to the people the "wisdom of the gods."

Fortunately, enough boys went in for the priestly profession, and their written exercises on clay were sufficiently durable, to provide historians with excellent examples of Sumerian grammar. Excavations at Ur, the most ancient city in the Tigris-Euphrates valley, have unearthed a schoolroom with its benches of hardened clay upon which sat the young scholars at their lessons. Their copybooks were oblong tablets of clay. On the left side was the teacher's model of writing; on the right, the boy carefully copied the signs, imprinting them with his reed stylus at an angle to the soft clay. What he learned by copying each day was dictated back to him the next day.

Learning to write was a hard task for a Sumerian boy. Instead of an alphabet of twenty-six letters, he had to learn more than five hundred symbols, each made by three to a dozen pricks of his stylus. His scratch pad, for practice writing, was a ball of clay that he moistened and flattened against a hard surface so that one side was smooth, like the underside of a cooky. When that surface became covered with writing, he would simply roll the clay back into a ball, knead it, flatten it out, and use it over again.

The *Babylonians*, as we know, conquered the Sumerians and took over their way of writing. They made many contributions of their own to knowledge: a correct calendar, measurements of time and space, and the division of numbers into fractions. Through the years they wrote thousands of books about these scientific subjects as well as others that were considered equally important, such as astronomy, astrology, and divination (prophecy by magic). The books, of course, were unwieldy—dried clay tablets intricately etched with cuneiform writing. It is hard to imagine reading them for pleasure. Yet on twelve such tablets was imprinted the first adventure story ever written, *The Epic of Gilgamesh*. Its hero was a legendary Babylonian king who, in his search for the secret of eternal life, grappled with fabulous beasts and villains and a great flood.

The great and greedy Assyrian king Ashurbanipal unwittingly performed a fine educational service for history. He had his officers collect all the tablet books in existence, to be copied by his scribes for his own library. It is said that there were at least 22,000 of them.

Since this king was a mighty warrior who spent much time attacking his neighboring countries, and a mighty hunter who boasted that he had slain no less than 370 lions, one wonders when he found time to enjoy his own library. But perhaps his scribes did his reading for him.

Egypt

Through his fingers, the child becomes great.

—HORI, an Egyptian writing teacher

Ancient Egyptians believed that the god Thoth had taught their early priests to write. This god was sometimes pictured as a man with the head of an ibis (a wading bird common to the banks of the Nile), and sometimes as a baboon—an animal, it must be added, that the Egyptians held sacred.

The early writing was done by word pictures called hieroglyphics, which means "sacred writing." Only the priests, their scribes, and a few enlightened nobles could read them. Indeed, nobles who could read were so proud of the accomplishment that they had themselves pictured holding a scroll, a mark of great honor. But to the great mass of people, the hieroglyphics were mysterious and holy.

As the years went on, professional scribes became more and more important in Egyptian affairs. Apart from serving the priests, they were useful in business. And the Egyptians were, above all, a busy people; like endless armies of ants, they built the great temples and vast pyramids that survive today. The

pyramids, of course, were tremendous feats of engineering—the largest, which covers 13 acres and towers 480 feet toward the sky, is said to have taken 220,000 men twenty years to build. As well as physical toil, such building required a knowledge of weights and measurements, force and balance, and all the other laws of construction. And besides these monumental projects, the Egyptians busied themselves with computing the rise and fall of the Nile, upon which they based their calendar; with planting and reaping their crops; with making bricks; with raising animals for food and work; with designing and making objects of art and household pottery, glass, leather goods and wooden utensils; and with buying and selling these things among themselves and with other nations.

All such activities required a great deal of paper work: records, instructions, accounts, correspondence. The efficient Egyptians loved paper work—perhaps because they had invented paper. They made it from the *papyrus*, a tall reedlike plant growing along the banks of the Nile. Papermakers extracted the core from this plant, pressed it into flat sheets, fastened a number of them together, and rolled them into scrolls which varied in length from 2 to 20 feet. Written scrolls were neatly stored in pottery jars for safekeeping.

Since paper work required people to read and write it, scribe schools were set up in the temples and the pharaoh's court. Boys (but no girls) could attend such a school in return for a small fee and a great willingness to learn. Only about five per cent of all Egyptian boys went to these schools; those who finished and became scribes were a privileged group. They were exempt from all the backbreaking labor that built the pyramids and tilled the soil. Even their food was provided from the royal storehouse.

"Put writing in thy heart," urged the priests, "so that thou mayest protect thine own person from any labor and be a respected official."

An Egyptian boy started scribe school at the age of four. It was well that he did so, for he had very much to learn. First, he had to master at least three different kinds of writing: the ancient hieroglyphic pictures of birds, beasts, serpents and everyday objects; the hieratic script, which resulted from writing such pictures swiftly with a brush; and the demotic, or popular, writing, an even quicker script used in everyday affairs. An older student might have to master the Babylonian cuneiform writing as well, and perhaps other foreign scripts, if he was preparing to go into foreign trade.

The three Egyptian scripts, however, were at least related to each other. They differed no more than our own print, our copybook writing, and the hurried scrawls many of us use today. And the Egyptians did make a wonderful contribution to writing that made their task much easier than that, say, of the Chinese. They discovered that, instead of making a different

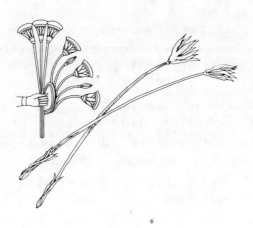

symbol for each word, they could represent words phonet-
ically by using symbols for sounds. The symbols which had
originally been *pictures* of words now expressed the *sounds* of
those words. For instance, the hieroglyph ⌐⌐ was the picture of a house. The Egyptian word for *house* starts with the
sound *p*; thus the symbol ⌐⌐ came to stand for *p*. The sign
⌐ meant *ro, mouth*; it came to represent simply the
consonant *r*. The symbol ⅋ was a word starting with the
sound of *ch* as in *chain*. With these signs, the Egyptians now
spelled their words. They did not use vowels; but, as in today's
shorthand system, they got on quite well without them. In case
there was any question as to what the consonants spelled, they
still put a hieroglyphic picture of the word beside it. Thus, if
we were to write English words using the above-mentioned
Egyptian symbols, ⅋ ⌐ ⌐ with a bird ⌇ beside it
would spell *chirp*—or, to be more accurate, we would write it
⌇ ⌐ ⌐ ⅋ , since the Egyptians wrote from right to left. In
writing of a baseball game, we would spell *pitcher* ⌇ ⌐ ⅋ ⌐
—to make sure that the reader did not think we meant ⌐ ⌐
⅋ ⌐ !

Thus, from hundreds of signs for words and syllables, Egyptian writing became simplified to a handy twenty-four symbols
for twenty-four consonant sounds. Before 1500 B.C. this phonetic writing was picked up by trading Phoenicians, was spread
to other countries by them, and became the basis for our own
alphabet.

Because the handmade papyrus paper was too precious to
waste, a boy first practiced writing on bits of broken pottery or
wood. His writing brush was a reed; his ink was made from red
or black earth mixed with gum and diluted with water. When
he had learned the principles of writing, he was given his own
scroll upon which to copy down his lessons.

School was held from dawn to dusk, and discipline was very
severe. "A boy's ears are on his back," says an old Egyptian
proverb, "and he hears only when he is beaten." Not that the
Egyptians were particularly cruel; they simply believed that

a boy, like a horse or a hawk, must be trained by force to do what was expected of him. Older boys who were lax in their studies were chained and put in prison cells until they were ready to mend their ways!

Plenty of time, too, was given to sports. Between sessions with their reeds and scrolls, boys went in for swimming, wrestling, stick fighting (dueling with sticks), weight-lifting, and even ball games—whose rules, unfortunately, we do not know, although pictures show us that Eyptian boys did play ball.

But the serious business of learning to write took many years. For many centuries the favorite textbook—or textscroll—was called *The Scribe of the Gods' Book*. It was compiled for students by Amenemope, a teacher at an advanced school called the House of Life. This book, he proudly explained, "instructs the ignorant to know everything that exists, what Ptah has created and Thoth has written, the heaven with all its stars, the earth and what is in it, what the mountains belch forth, and what flows from the ocean, all things which the sun sheds a light upon and all that grows in the earth." There follows list upon list of all things known to the Egyptians: sun, moon, different stars, winds and storms; the titles of rulers, officials, and other persons, and the different classes of society; kinds of buildings and architectural terms; all known cities; all known birds and beasts and fishes; all kinds of foods—including thirty-three different meat dishes! The students had to learn the symbols for these as well as the spelling of all these words.

When he was about ten years old, now the proud possessor of his own scroll, the boy copied in it the things he would keep on using as references. There were passages of prose that he had to learn by heart to improve his style; the various forms of elegant letters to be used in writing to a government official, or even to the pharaoh himself; and his lessons in geography, morals, and mathematics.

His way of doing arithmetic seems to us absurdly awkward. But it must be remembered that the Egyptians were in the process of discovering the rules of mathematics and what they knew had been figured out from observation and practical sense. Instead of multiplying, they counted the way a small child counts on his fingers. They had few symbols to represent numbers. A boy learned to write 1 as 1 , 2 as 11 , 3 as $\overset{11}{1}$, and so on. A hundred was expressed by ☺ ; 400 was ☺☺☺☺ . The figure for 1,000 was beautiful and mysterious ☥ ; it was merely repeated for as many thousands as were needed.

But even with this roundabout way of dealing with numbers, the Egyptian scholar learned to solve quite difficult problems in what we now call algebra and geometry.

His principal science was astronomy. The Egyptians had mapped the heavens with accuracy and used the phases of the moon and the passing of the seasons to predict the overflowing of the Nile—the annual event that, in that dry country, meant a season of enriched soil and irrigation for the crops.

His geography was limited but important. While nothing was known about the vast expanses of our Western world and no more than rumors about the Far East, the ships and caravans of trade had brought Egypt a knowledge of Phoenicia, Syria, Crete, Palestine, Greece, and Mesopotamia—faraway lands to the studying youth, but exciting, and important to his country's commerce.

Throughout all his studies, the boy was strictly schooled in his behavior. He had to learn to conduct himself as befitted a man of letters. To this end, he copied and learned by heart many moral precepts, such as "greater is the appeal of the gentle than of the strong,"—a thought that may have surprised him after all those floggings! He learned to be respectful, even subservient. He had to be worshipfully grateful to his mother for raising him. He had to be concerned for the welfare of all women—particularly, of course, widows, who seem to have been especially treasured throughout history. He also had to learn to wipe envy from his heart and to be proud of his lot, even though he was constantly urged to improve it. And he had to learn all sorts of correct manners, including proper deportment at table. "When he gives to thee, take what he puts before thee; but do not look at what is before him, look at what is before thee" was a formal rule for keeping your eyes on your own dinner.

When he reached the age of thirteen or fourteen, the schoolboy might become an apprentice, or student worker, in his chosen profession.

Or he might continue his studies with the teaching priests, with a view of going into the priesthood, or government, or medicine. This last profession took real courage, for the law was that if a patient died, the doctor was subject to capital punishment! But it was a respected profession, requiring then, as now, much study. The man of medicine not only had to know all the rules for driving the demons of disease from the patient's body; he had to know how to exterminate rats, mice, and insects; how to treat mosquito bites and baldness; and how to concoct such precious creams and cosmetics as were used by Cleopatra to lure Mark Antony to his fate.

Important positions in government awaited the youths who completed their studies at the court school for scribes. Such a graduate might become an army officer or "royal scribe of the army," or a cavalry officer, a "scribe of the royal stables." Or he might be appointed "grain scribe of Upper and Lower Egypt" (minister of agriculture) or "scribe of the house of silver" (secretary of the treasury).

A famous court school was called the School of Sesostris, named after a young prince of the court. His proud father had offered free tuition to all little boys who were born on the same day as Sesostris, and later to other bright, ambitious boys throughout the kingdom. This school may well have been the forerunner of other free court schools, which we shall come upon later.

The School of Sesostris was rigorous. It is said that the boys were made to run 20 miles each day before breakfast. Perhaps the Egyptian mile was shorter than ours.

India

*Let us think on the lovely splendor
of the god Savitri
that he may inspire our minds.*

—from the Rig-Veda, 1500 B.C. (?)

India, too, had schools during the thousand years before Christ. But these schools were as different from those of Egypt as they were far away from that practical land.

Knowledge, to the people of ancient India, was not of the "how to" sort. It was not concerned with how to build or how to make things or how to do business—or even very much with how to read and write. It was the lore of philosophy, of deep thought, and of spiritual values. Its texts were the four Vedas—collections of poetry and prose which for many hundreds of years were passed on orally, not written down. The words were held fast in the minds of teachers, who taught them only to pupils of their own choosing.

These teachers, called gurus, were gentle, almost saintly men. According to ancient rules, a teacher must be "of gentle speech; [who] even when offended, never offends by word; never injures another by thought or deed; and who never, under penalty of losing heaven, makes others fear him by word or act."

34

The guru could afford to be gentle, for the boys whom he accepted as students were not the sort who would need beating or punishment. They were chosen for their character, intelligence, and eagerness to serve their teacher. They were prepared to pactice great self-discipline as part of their education.

The students left their homes to live at a sort of primitive boarding school. The schoolhouse, or *tol*, was a one-room house in which the guru lived and held his classes. Surrounding the tol were simple mud huts for his pupils. These huts kept out the heavy tropical rains of India, but otherwise they were not comfortable—nor were they meant to be. A thin rug for sleeping, a pot for cooking, a bowl for food, and perhaps a brush and parchment for writing—these were all the furnishings. Students' minds were not supposed to dwell on creature comforts but upon their studies and their service to their teacher.

Part of such service was to beg for food and money to support themselves. Indeed, the entire school was supported by begging, for the pupils ate only what the master chose to leave them.

A code of laws, although it was not written down until later, gives us an idea of the life at a guru's school:

A professed student shall serve his master unto death.
A professed student shall bridle his tongue.
He shall eat in the fourth, sixth, or eighth hour of the day.
He shall go out in order to beg.
He shall obey his teacher.
If his teacher walks, he shall attend him while walking after him; if his teacher is sitting, while standing; if his teacher lies down, while seated.
He must bathe three times a day.

Thus surrounded by tender loving care, the guru initiated his pupils into the mysteries of wisdom. Their first lessons were in the proper performance of the *sandhya*, a set of religious rites to be carried out each morning, noon, and evening. These devotions were made up of prayers, singing, and rhythmical breath control, accompanied by a ritual sipping of water and libations poured to the sun.

When the boys had mastered these, they were set to work on the Vedas, four books of wisdom and praise that the teacher had learned by heart. Seated on the ground with his pupils crouched around him, the guru expounded these mystical books. Word by word, sentence by sentence, verse by verse, for hours each day, the boys repeated the master's words until they too could recite them by heart.

They learned about the beginning of the world, its gods and goddesses, and man's duty toward perfection. They learned some fascinating notions: that the world was a vast room outlined in space, with the sky held above it by poles, like a marquee, and the earth fixed in space by pegs, with the god Brihaspati holding up its ends. They learned, too, some "history": accounts of wars and conquering tribes that probably had some basis in fact. Most of this lore came from singing poetry, interspersed with many hymns of praise to the gods.

Since poetry is easier to remember than prose, perhaps this learning by rote was not too difficult. The schoolboys, however, not only had to recite the verses but also had to ponder deeply on their meaning. And since the Vedas were in a language that was already outdated, their meaning was a challenge. To interpret them properly required six more subjects called the "limbs of the Veda." These studies covered the correct forms of sacrifices, the proper pronunciation of Vedic words, the study of its meters, the derivations of its words, the formation of its grammar, and the science of astronomy as set forth in its myths.

There was no accelerated course in the Vedas. It took a student twelve years to master one book. Those who learned all four, in order to become teachers themselves, kept at it for forty-eight years.

Surely, after all this, the gurus deserved to be waited on by their own pupils.

Early Synagogue Schools

Our principal care of all is this, to educate our children well; and we think it to be the most necessary business of our whole life, to observe the laws that have been given to us, and to keep those rules of piety that have been delivered to us.

—JOSEPHUS

The first children who were required by law to go to school were Jewish boys. In 175 B.C. Simon ben-Shetach, a high priest of Jerusalem, ordered that the synagogues in that city open their schools to all boys—and that all boys attend them. Whether a boy was rich or poor, lazy or industrious, ambitious or easygoing, his parents had to send him to the synagogue for his education.

Not until two thousand years later did the Western world take up the idea of free compulsory schooling for every child.

The synagogue schools were primarily for teaching religion. The Jewish people were the first to worship one God, one great and all-embracing Heavenly Father, rather than the many and often capricious deities of other peoples. They held their religion to be the most important thing in their lives—and with reason. Throughout a long, hard history of conquest by other nations, of capture and bondage and scattering of their tribes in foreign lands, it was the religion of the Jews and their persistence in teaching it to their children that held them together as a people. They believed that they were the one people chosen by God to carry his truth through the ages. To them, therefore, *wisdom* meant the knowledge of God's word as written down by their high priests. History and literature were limited to the Bible. Music consisted of religious chants. And *law* meant the rules for virtuous living as set down by Moses and the prophets.

The little boys started school, as now, at the age of six. They had already had some teaching at home; they could probably repeat some psalms and proverbs from the Bible as well as the Ten Commandments. Now they had to learn to read and write, to count and add a little, and to recite long passages from the Pentateuch, the first five books of the Bible.

Every day throughout the year except on the Sabbath, school was held from dawn to dusk, with a short recess at noon. The boys sat in a row on the ground—or on wooden benches, if they were to be had—but always facing the teacher, for this was one of the Biblical rules. "And though the Lord shall give you the bread of adversity, and the water of affliction, yet shall not thy teachers be removed into the corner any more, but thine eyes shall see thy teachers," wrote the prophet Isaiah; and the rule-abiding Jews took this as a literal command to keep their eyes on the teacher's face.

Next to the high priests, the teachers, or rabbis, were the most revered persons in all Israel.

"You should revere the teacher more than your father," says the Talmud, the book of sacred laws. "The latter only brought you into this world; the former shows the way to the next."

The rabbis showed the way by means of the "loud school" method of teaching, like that of the Chinese and the Indians. Page after page of the Bible, list after list of moral precepts were shouted aloud by the boys in their effort to learn them by heart. This relentless diet of learning by rote was the fare not only in all ancient schools but in schools for many hundreds of years

after. The rabbis, however, made some humane effort to make the memorizing easier. They arranged much of the material into *atbash*, a mystical system of alphabetizing, listing the laws so as to start with consecutive letters of the alphabet.

The alphabet used at this time was the same one that had been handed over by the Egyptians to the voyaging Phoenicians, who brought it to Israel. The boys practiced their letters by pressing a stylus on a tablet of wax—for here, as in other countries, paper was much too precious to be wasted on children. Only older youths who were writing down things worth keeping were awarded the papyrus scroll and the ink for writing on it.

In spite of the improved alphabet, reading had its special difficulties for boys at the synagogue schools. For the Pentateuch, their principal textbook, was written in ancient Hebrew —a language no longer in daily use at that time. And it was strictly forbidden to translate or alter a word of the old sacred text. So boys—and even girls, who were often taught at home —like the Indian students, had to learn to read and understand an antiquated language. They had to read it, moreover, with true reverence for the holy word and with right expression and good diction—requirements that could do with some attention in our schools today.

For arithmetic, the boys learned to count and to write down numbers on their wax tablets. And here they were fortunate, for their system of writing numerals was beautifully simple:

Numbers 1 through 9 were expressed by the first nine letters of the alphabet. The next group of nine letters stood for numbers 10, 20, and so on through 90. The third group of nine letters expressed the hundreds, 100 through 900. The letters were combined to form combinations of numbers. Thus, if we were to use this means of expressing numbers with our modern alphabet, we would write that KD hours make a day; G days make a week; and NB weeks or UOE days make a year!

There is no record of games or sports or, indeed, any physical exercises in the synagogue schools—only the long school day with its short recess at noon. Discipline was severe; the rod stood in the corner ready to help the lazy boy along the path to the next world.

"Thou shalt beat him with a rod to deliver his soul from hell" was the rule, for it was a firm belief that children were born willful and should have the fear of the Lord beaten into them. Fathers were urged to carry on the strict discipline at home. "He that spareth his rod hateth his son," said the proverb, "but he that loveth him chasteneth him betimes." And, "Chasten thy son while there is hope," warned another, "and let not thy soul spare him for his crying."

Fifteen hundred years later, New Englanders boiled such precepts down to the simple adage, "Spare the rod and spoil the child." The fact that so many Jewish proverbs urged punishment leads one to suspect that Jewish parents, if left to themselves, were inclined to be overlenient.

The synagogue schools of Jerusalem, strict as they were and limited as to subjects, produced the first *literate* people in history. The Jews were the first nation whose men of all classes could read and write.

And in A.D. 64 the rabbi Joshua ben Gemala extended this rule of compulsory schooling throughout all of Palestine. "A town without scholars and school children should be destroyed," he said, and forbade families to live in such a town. He went on to become a sort of board of education all by himself, laying down rules for the size of classes and number of teachers: for more than twenty-five pupils, the teacher must have an assistant; for a school of forty, there must be two teachers; and so on.

This great and good rabbi even gave orders for the education of girls! He advised a combined course in religion and household duties for those hitherto neglected creatures. He did not, however, go so far as to suggest that girls should go to school. Perhaps, like many educators, he wanted to be sure of his comforts at home.

"The Glory That Was Greece"

Meanwhile, long before ben-Shetach and the synagogue schools, the Greek civilization was in its golden age. It was a civilization whose radiance has lit the world ever since. The very phrase "classical Greece" calls up a picture of sunlight on marble temples, of singing sculptures, of music and poetry, of brave deeds, of surging ideals, and of the birth of democracy.

In that "democratic" society, however, only about one-third of the boys had the privilege of schooling. These were the sons of "citizens," men of good family who owned land and had a voice in government. Half of the population were slaves—men, women, and children who performed all the manual labor and had no rights whatsoever. A third class were the metics, or foreigners, who might run businesses if they wished—a pursuit that was held to be beneath the dignity of citizens—but who had no vote or educational privileges.

This class system was the same in the two great city-states of Athens and Sparta. But in the schooling of their young citizens they were as different from each other as they were from the Hebrews.

SPARTA

The Spartan boy's life belonged to the state. In about 800 B.C.

the lawgiver Lycurgus had made the rules for his education—and, indeed, for his entire life up to the age of sixty.

As soon as he was born, he was bathed in wine—not as a form of celebration, but to give him strength. Then, loosely wrapped, he was taken to the governing Council of Elders for inspection. The Council looked him over carefully to decide whether he was worth raising. If he was sickly, he would be taken to the mountainside and abandoned there, left to die of exposure or to be eaten by wild beasts. But if he passed inspection, his mother was allowed to keep him until he was seven years old. She trained him not to cry, to endure hunger and discomfort, and never to show fear of anything.

At seven he was taken from home and put in a sort of boarding school. His parents had to pay for his provisions while he was there; if they failed to do so, they ceased to be citizens.

His school was more like an army camp than a place for study. It was a sort of barracks. The boys were divided into groups of sixty-four, each group under an *eren*, a youth who had turned twenty. The eren was assisted by the bravest and most prudent boys in his group to keep order. Each group slept on the floor of one large room on "beds" that were no more than a thin layer of reeds gathered by the boys themselves. They were allowed no blankets—such comforts were held to be weakening; but in wintertime they could add some thistle-down to their reeds to keep out drafts from the floor.

Their feet were bare, and their hair was cut close to harden their heads to heat and cold alike. When they were twelve years old, and supposedly tough and strong enough, their clothing was reduced to one garment, a tunic like a short dress, in which they lived and slept for a full year before being given a new one. The boys of each group ate together, but sparingly, for the Spartans believed that much food stunted a boy's growth! They drilled, wrestled, and shot arrows together, all under constant supervision, with no hours off to themselves. Their bath was an occasional dip in the Eurotas river flowing beside the city. They were dirty, obedient, and very, very brave.

And what were the lessons that the Spartan boy learned at his school? Not book learning; he was given no books. Instead he was taught the requirements of good citizenship as set down by Lycurgus: strength, endurance, courage, patriotism, military efficiency, and cunning. He was trained to run, to leap, to wrestle, to throw the discus and the javelin.

Even though these exercises sound like sports, they were not carried on with the idea of having a good time. Each exercise was planned, like calisthenics, to improve the boy's body; throwing a ball was not a game but an exercise to strengthen the muscles of his arm. Not that there was any rule against enjoying the exercises; one imagines that the boys, being fit to begin with, enjoyed them thoroughly. They were taught that to serve the state as good soldiers was their highest goal, and they were immensely proud of their discipline and fitness. And if a boy was inclined to be lax—well, he was soon found out. Every ten days the group paraded naked before the governing elders. And if any boy showed a tendency to soft muscle, an official whip bearer "encouraged" him to better effort.

As part of their training, Spartan boys were sent out on forays to the surrounding countryside. There they were to pick up food, firewood, and other necessities as best they could— usually by stealing. And woe betide the boy who got caught, for that spelled shame. The famous little Spartan boy who, having stolen a fox, let it gnaw his vitals rather than confess was only choosing the more immediate of two punishments.

A favorite project for older boys was *cryptia*, a game of hiding in ambush to pounce on the enemy. This "enemy," so-called, was the unfortunate class of Helots, the slave farmers who tilled the soil on the outskirts of the town and were considered fair game for the marauding boys.

The Spartans have often been called brainless. There was little to encourage the intellect in this military kind of schooling. They were supposed to learn their letters, but time was not wasted on reading. Their literature was the laws of Lycurgus, which they learned to chant aloud. Writing was not required;

in fact the Spartans felt that writing things down served only to weaken the memory. There were warlike passages from Homer which the boys learned by heart to improve their sense of patriotism. And there were battle songs to rouse their ardor for combat. They had dancing, too: a series of warlike motions, like a drill, set to strict and solemn chords on the seven-stringed lyre.

The boys' behavior at all times was silent and dignified. They walked with their hands in their sleeves, their eyes cast down and unswerving. When spoken to, they must answer quickly; when asked a question, they were to answer politely in as few words as possible. In fact this brevity of speech—which is still called "laconic" after the Spartan province of Laconia—was a great specialty of the well-trained Spartan youth. A favorite contest in the evenings, after the frugal dinner, was to outdo each other in such terse speech. The eren would ask the boys questions about some weighty topic, such as who was the city's most admirable man and why, or what would be the proper thing to do in such and such a situation. In answering, a boy must not hesitate or stammer or beat about the bush. His answer must be swift, brief, and to the point. If it was not—if an "er" or "I mean" crept in, his forfeit was to have his thumbs bitten by the eren—a prospect only a little less painful than a fox in the tunic.

Boys continued this military schooling until they were eighteen. At that age they were inducted into the army as recruits, swearing their oath of allegiance to the state.

For two more years they underwent an even stiffer training. They were sent out on practice maneuvers, sleeping on the bare ground and foraging for food as best they could. At twenty they became regular soldiers and spent the next ten years fighting wars; or, if there was no war on, harassing those unfortunate Helots on the pretext that they were plotting to revolt.

At thirty, the Spartan was considered to have reached manhood. He was now ordered to marry—though his elders must approve the match. But even after marriage, he continued to spend most of his time at the public barracks, overseeing the training of the young boys, while his wife took care of the children at home.

Spartan women did not resent this arrangement. They too had been brought up to worship the military state. Their girlhood was spent in physical training almost as rigorous as their brothers'. Even though they lived at home, they formed groups to learn drill, to run and leap, to hurl the discus and the javelin, and even to wrestle with the boys. And they joined the boys in the symbolic warrior dances held in public places to amuse and impress the populace.

Spartan girls were taught to be better athletes than housewives. After all, they had plenty of slaves to wait on them in the home. And, too, there was not much point learning the arts of homemaking when the menfolk spent most of their lives in the barracks.

ATHENS

The young Athenian, unlike the Spartan boy, did not belong to the state. He belonged to his father, who, if the latter decided to keep him, raised him with pride and paid for his education.

Until he was six or seven, the little Athenian played at home with his parents and young brothers and sisters. But when school days started, his life changed. He was put in the charge of a pedagogue, an elderly trusted slave who acted as a sort of male governess, helping the boy to dress, correcting his manners, hearing his lessons, and escorting him to and from the various teachers who now took over his days. From now on, although he still lived at home, his life was quite separate from his family.

At dawn the schoolboy was awakened by his pedagogue. He "washed the sleep from his eyes," as the writer Lucian put it, and put on his clothes: the comfortable short tunic belted at the waist, the sandals laced high on his legs, the cloak which he wore on the street. After a light breakfast the two set forth, the pedagogue carrying the boy's "book" and writing materials

and the lyre for his music lesson. The old man walked a step behind his pupil, all the while keeping an eye on his behavior; for the young Athenian, like the Spartan, had to walk with downcast eyes, erectly, but not too fast—for haste, to the Athenians, was bad form. Thus, strolling sedately through the early light, they came to the house of the grammatist, who taught the boy reading, writing, and sometimes counting.

There were no grades in the Athenian boy's school. The various teachers took on a few boys at a time, teaching each at his own pace. A boy was not supposed to dawdle; either the teacher or the pedagogue could use the rod if he was lazy. However, because of the Athenian ideal of moderation in everything, the student's lessons were neither very difficult nor monotonous. They were planned with a view to making him a good citizen rather than a scholar.

Reading and writing began with learning the letters. The Greek alphabet was an adaptation of the Phoenician alphabet, which, in turn, was adapted from the Egyptian one. The boy's "copybook" was made of two pieces of wood attached together by leather thongs, their inner surfaces coated with wax. His pen was a metal stylus, pointed at one end for writing, rounded at the other for erasing by smoothing over the wax so that the "page" could be used over and over again. The teacher first cut the letters into the wax for the beginner, so that, by tracing them over with his stylus, he learned their shapes. Soon he was writing words by himself, and what he wrote down on one day, he read back on the next. In spite of all his care in forming the letters, it was hard to read his own writing—or anyone else's, for that matter. The Greeks used no capitals to mark the beginnings of sentences, no punctuation, no spacing even between words to show where one stopped and the next began. The grammatist helped him, however, by marking the boy's copy into words and sentences for easier reading.

When he could read and write well enough, the student was given his own scroll of parchment, ink of lampblack and gum, and a metal pen. His writings were now passages of poetry dictated by the teacher. It has been said that while boys of other nations were taught by priests, Athenian boys were taught by the poets; and indeed the Greeks looked to their poets for their ideals. The favorite was Homer, the legendary blind poet whose epics sang the heroic history of Greece. The poems were not only beautifully written, they were filled with high thoughts and deeds. The grammatist, by teaching boys to read, write, and recite them, merely opened the works of the poets to his pupils; it was from the poems themselves that the students learned history, and geography, and courage, and beauty, and love of country.

From writing and reading it over again, the boy learned much of Homer by heart. The more Homer he could recite, the higher his education. One proud father claimed that his son could recite all of Homer—which, if true, was quite a feat, since the *Odyssey* and the *Iliad* run to hundreds of pages.

From the grammatist, too, the boy learned arithmetic. He did not have to learn much of it, for Greek citizens were not

expected to know much mathematics. Since aristocrats did not work at a business or profession, they felt no need for their sons to know more than how to count a few things—their money, their slaves, the measurements of their houses and lands. There were no written figures for numbers. The word for the number was written out—as if the number 21 could only be expressed by writing *twenty-one*.

Like all peoples, the Greeks had started out by counting on their fingers. They continued to think of numbers in multiples of fives and tens, as is shown on the ingenious board used for teaching arithmetic.

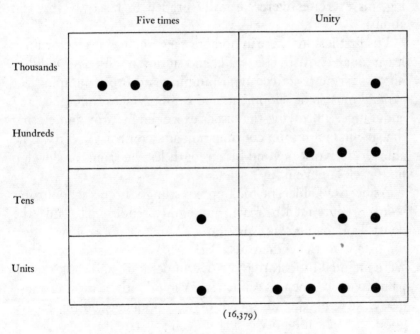

(16,379)

The board was divided into eight spaces, each housing a number or its multiple. Pebbles placed in the different spaces represented units, or their multiples in fives, tens, hundreds, or thousands. Thus each pebble in the lower right-hand space was 1; each in the upper-left-hand space was 5,000. This may seem a cumbersome way to do sums, but no doubt the Greeks found it useful.

After a few hours of these lessons, the boy and his pedagogue went on to the *palaestra*, a private gymnasium for boys. The Athenians insisted on a graceful and well-formed physique; fully half a schoolboy's time was spent in physical education.

On entering the palaestra, he saluted the *paedotribe* (the athletics instructor), paid his respects to a statue of Hermes, the god of athletics, and took off his clothes for the pedagogue to keep while he exercised. In the gymnasium were boys of different ages and sizes; enough were of his own age for competitive games. But again, each boy had individual instruction from the paedotribe. Instead of the Spartan routine of mere muscle building, his exercises were carefully graded to his own size and ability.

His first lessons were in bodily grace, such as any actor must learn today: how to rise, walk, and sit down with ease and dignity. Next he practiced high jumping and broad jumping for general muscle development, and running races for agility and endurance. Throwing the discus exercised his arm, and casting the javelin taught him coordination and control. Never was he allowed to work beyond his strength lest he strain or develop his muscles unevenly.

As he grew older, he took up wrestling with his schoolmates —a sport intended to teach him agility, endurance, and "the control of tempers and passions." This self-control was very important to the Athenians. Perhaps, as an artistic race, they were inclined by nature to be overimpetuous, and took special pains to overcome this tendency. A good citizen must not lose his temper or take advantage of his opponent; he must have good manners and good control in all sports.

After his lessons in athletics, the boy had a bath, and perhaps a swimming lesson, if his palaestra was near the river. Athenian boys were taught early to swim for reasons of cleanliness as well as exercise. Then he dressed and was escorted home for his midday meal—"not too large," explains the writer Lucian, "for the schoolmasters are waiting for him again, and the books which teach him who was a great hero, who was a lover of justice and purity."

Since our young student has had his reading, writing, and counting lessons in the morning, he goes in the afternoon to the *cithariste*, or teacher of music. Music, to the Athenians, was not merely one of the arts. It was an important part of their lives. Music and poetry were intertwined. Poetry, to be properly rendered, was accompanied by music; and since poetry sang of ideals, of heroes, of valor and of purity, music was part of its language. Athenians had a talent for drama; they used music to set a mood of reverence, or of action, or of tenderness. Boys who later would dance in patriotic and religious festivals learned the uses of music while they were still young. The simple Dorian mode (e–c–b–a–f–e) was held to be most suitable for use by schoolboys, as was the seven-stringed lyre, although other instruments were sometimes taught. The philosopher Plato, writing a few years later, argued against the harp as being too difficult for a youth to manage, and against the flute as being too exciting (as well as unbecoming to the boy's face as he puffed out his cheeks to blow it!).

His lessons in music and poetry over, the boy had time for more games. Usually he went back to the palaestra to play ball or prisoner's base, or to compete with his friends at running races.

But no school or gymnasium could be open after dark. All boys and their pedagogues had to be off the streets and in their own homes by sundown. At dusk, then, the schoolboy and the patient old man set out for home—where, as Lucian writes, "he pays the necessary tribute to his stomach and retires to rest, to sleep sweetly after his busy day" until dawn, when the school day started all over again, seven days a week (except for some ninety festival days scattered throughout the year).

When a boy turned sixteen, he was considered to have had enough education to be called a gentleman and could quit school if his family wished. But to become a full-fledged citizen, with a voice in the government, he had to spend four more years in learning.

Now, however, the young man's schooling took a different turn. No longer did the pedagogue dog his footsteps, carrying his things and tending his manners. He was allowed to go about Athens alone. In his free time he could attend theaters or trials, or talk with the grown men in the market place about the topics of the day. But if ever he abused his privileges by raucous or unseemly behavior, he would be called up before the state officials for punishment.

His athletic training now became more intense. He spent most of his days at one of the state gymnasiums. There were three of these: one for the aristocrats, one for those families who had recently become citizens, and one for those families who, alas, were partly of foreign blood. In these gymnasiums, set beside the river for swimming and open to the sky for air and sunshine, the young men of Athens gathered for their exercises; the older ones, to watch, to bathe, to discuss the affairs of the day. The young man's exercises were more strenuous than the boy's; the discus and javelin were heavier; the jumps were higher and wider; the races were run with the contestants dressed in armor.

His wrestling, too, was now a serious matter. He was coated with oil and sprinkled with sand for the ordeal—after which he scraped it all off with a bone instrument, called the *strigil*, before his plunge into the river.

At eighteen, if he had acquitted himself well, the young Athenian became an *ephebos*, or citizen-cadet. This was a great milestone in his life and was attended by a solemn ritual. His father took him before the state officials, who looked into his birth, his morals, and his physique; and if he passed muster, he was registered as a prospective citizen. His hair, which had previously been worn somewhat long, was now cut short; he was given the dark cloth garment worn by citizens to distinguish them from lesser folk. In a public ceremony he was presented to the people of the city, was awarded a shield and spear, and was escorted to the temple. There, with due reverence, he took the ephebic oath:

I will never disgrace these sacred arms, nor desert the comrades at my side. I will fight for temples and public property, both alone and with others. I will pass along the heritage of my country not less, but greater, than it was passed on to me. I will obey the magistrates who at any time may be in authority. I will obey both the laws which now exist, and those which may hereafter be made by the people; and if any person seeks to annul the laws or set them at naught, I will do my best to prevent him, and will defend them both by myself and with others. I will honor the religion of my fathers. And I call to my witness the gods Agraulos, Enyalios, Ares, Zeus, Thallo, Auxo, and Hegemone.

For two years the youth served as an ephebos, a sort of soldier sent about the countryside to learn its geography and its means of defense, to help preserve order by patrolling its borders, and to serve in any way needed by the state. At the end of that term, if he had performed his duties faithfully, he became a full-fledged citizen.

"And the Grandeur
That Was Rome"

There is a well-known picture on the wall of a ruin in Herculaneum of a Roman schoolboy being thrashed with a bundle of switches before the downcast eyes of his schoolmates.

The painting has given many of us the idea that Roman schools were particularly harsh. But there is no reason to believe that Roman discipline was more strict than in other ancient schools. The Romans, in fact, were especially fond of their children and took much care in their upbringing.

Long before schools were started, the Roman father educated his sons himself, teaching them to read and count, taking them on the rounds of his farm, or keeping them by his side as he went about his civic duties, discussing and deciding matters of state with his fellow citizens. For the Romans, like the Egyptians, were a practical people. While the Greek boy was learning to chant poetry and move with grace, the Roman boy was learning about crops and laws and the building of roads.

But as Rome conquered more and more parts of Greece and brought home numbers of educated Greeks as captives, she caught on to the idea of schools. And soon Roman children—girls as well as boys—were flocking to school in the care of Greek slave pedagogues.

Roman schools were more efficient than those of the Greeks. The children were taught in classes—not so large as those of to-day, for not nearly so many children went to school, but large enough so that six to ten youngsters were learning the same thing at the same time. The subjects, too, were more down to earth. No music—the Romans did not have the Greek passion for music. No physical grace or athletic exercises in the palaes-tra—these to the Romans were a waste of time. The use-ful subjects of reading, writing, and computing, and of law, business, and public speaking—these were the studies required for a practical education.

At the age of seven, then, the young Romans set out at dawn to attend the *ludus*, or elementary school. Fewer girls than boys went to school. Both sexes wore white robes trimmed with purple, a costume that the girls continued to wear until they were married. The pedagogue carried the child's school things in a sort of schoolbag called a *capsa*. This was a cylindrical box which held his metal pen, his roll of parchment, and the bag of pebbles, or *calculi*, which he used for arithmetic.

The schoolroom might be the porch of a house, or a room in a shop, or a shed, or any other convenient empty spot. It was furnished with a chair and table for the teacher, and wooden benches without backs for the pupils. Next to it was a small anteroom for the waiting pedagogues, the cloaks, and the *ferula* —the bundle of switches awaiting the unruly.

More often than not the teacher was a slave—a Greek captured in war who had more learning than his captors. His fee for teaching was a polite "present" from the student's family—but a present whose value had already been agreed upon before the student was accepted. If the *ludus magister,* or primary-school teacher, was a citizen-owned slave, he turned his fees over to his master.

Reading and writing lessons were very much like those of the Athenian boy. The alphabet had been borrowed from the Greeks and was used with few changes. And the young Romans were taught to read Homer, whose works had been translated into their native Latin by Livius Andronicus, a captured Greek who was given his freedom for this welcome service. They learned and loved the tales of Aesop, the deformed and beloved slave who was also freed by his admiring master. Roman boys also studied the "Laws of the Twelve Tables," which set forth the famous Roman system of justice, the basis of law courts ever since. Their copybooks, like those of the Athenians and the Hebrews, were wax tablets; when they could write legibly, they had their parchment *dictata* on which to set down their permanent writings.

Arithmetic was a more serious business for the Roman boy than for the Greek, for a Roman citizen was expected to be a good businessman. He started out with the "finger reckoning" used by merchants in the market place. The fingers on his left hand expressed numbers up to 10; those on his right hand, tens and hundreds. The motions of the merchants' hands were swift. The Roman boy had to be expert at this finger arithmetic, for a man who fumbled at it was looked upon as illiterate!

For written sums the Roman numerals were awkward, to say

the least. Those numerals—I, II, III, IV, V, VI, VII, VIII, IX, X, L, C, D, M—are of course still in use today. But it is obvious that they are difficult to add and subtract, and even more difficult to divide and multiply.

The Roman counting board, upon which the boys worked sums with their reckoning pebbles, was somewhat advanced over that of the Greeks. It looked like this:

MILLIONS	THOUSANDS			HUNDREDS	TENS	UNITS
M	C	X	I	C	X	I
8,	7	6	0,	2	5	4

On this board, pebbles above the dividing line stood for 5 times those below it. Only those pebbles placed near the dividing line counted; the rest were spares, to be used as needed. To indicate 3 in the right-hand unit column, one of the four pebbles would be pushed down. To indicate 5, all would be pushed down, and a pebble from above placed at the "five times" line. To show 6, one pebble would be moved up beneath it (but below the line); to show 7, two pebbles; and so on. The number 10, of course, would become one pebble in the 10 column. If you examine this board, you will see that the columns are from right to left in multiples of ten, as we arrange numbers today. The "carrying" was simply done by moving pebbles. This counting board was the forerunner of the *abacus*, which, instead of pebbles, has beads strung on wires. It is still in use in some Oriental countries today and is said to be a very swift way of totaling numbers.

At the age of ten or eleven, girls stopped going to the *ludus* and were taught at home by their mothers. But boys, if they were lucky enough to afford it, went on to the *grammaticus*, or grammar-school teacher, who plunged them deep into grammar.

Roman citizens had reason to be concerned about grammar. Many different tribes had come to Italy—Indo-Europeans, Etruscans, Greeks, Gauls, Egyptians, Jews—all speaking as many different tongues. In a society like that of Rome, where only a few had the privilege of learning to read at all, such peoples talked in broken language, trying as best they could to make themselves understood. By making a science of their own tongue, its spelling and correct use, the Romans solidified it into the classical Latin that has come down to us as the model of clarity and beauty of expression. The boys learned their grammar rules orally until they knew them by heart. The only textbook belonged to the teacher.

Along with grammar came the art of reading poetry correctly. As more recent generations of students have been only too well aware, the structure of Latin poetry is subtle; it is essential to its beauty to scan it properly, giving the syllables and pauses their proper values. One might say that Latin verse has its own built-in music, needing no accompanying lyre to make it sing. But it does need care in reading.

The Roman script did not make the task easier. With its letters all in capitals, crowded together, and with little or no punctuation, it took some deciphering to read it at all, let alone with the required gusto. But the young Roman mastered it; and learned to read the translated Homer, as well as Vergil's epic of the "pious Aeneas" and other Latin works intended to teach him history and heroism and manly virtue.

His diet of language and literature was varied with a bit of science—geometry and astronomy. But his geometry, which literally means "earth measuring," was little more than that at the time. It was a sort of geography and map making. Its results were more fascinating than accurate.

His "astronomy," too, was amusing (to us, if not to him). He was taught that the earth was flat, and that the heavenly bodies revolved around it—all of which he could see for himself by standing outdoors at night. But it would be practical, it was felt, for him to learn more about the moon and stars in order to measure the seasons of the year. He was therefore taught to "read" the skies and interpret not only lightning as the wrath of Jupiter, but other signs that would influence the planting and harvesting of crops.

Although physical education, as such, was not part of schooling, Roman boys were certainly encouraged to be active and healthy. They had their playtimes and games; they played ball and learned to swim and ride horseback, as will boys of all times when given the chance.

They took a more active part in family life, and even in public life, than had the sheltered young Athenians. The Romans had many occasions for family ceremonies—a funeral or the honoring of an important relative. Such ceremonies were led by the father as head of the clan, and the boys took pride in assisting him. In public religious festivals, too, the boys played gratifying roles. They carried torches, strewed flowers, and chanted hymns as they marched in the procession.

At sixteen, the young Roman put off his purple-trimmed boy's dress and was given the *toga virilis*, the garment of a grown-up citizen. This was a semicircular cape, generally made of wool and dyed a rich, bright color. Draped over the tunic and with its right end tossed over the left shoulder, it gave the Roman citizen his fine, bulky appearance as he strode down the street or sat in the senate.

Upon receiving his toga, a boy could stop school without being considered a dropout. He was now looked upon as an educated citizen. But if he and his family wished—and particularly if he planned to hold some public office—he went on to the school of the *rhetor*, the teacher of rhetoric.

At the time the Romans conquered Greece, they found that Athenian education had largely fallen into the hands of Sophists, philosophers who were great arguers and speechifiers. The Romans particularly admired this art of oratory; and indeed, in the days when so few people could read and write, to be able to sway a crowd was a useful art. One Greek orator named Prohaeresius was said to be such a persuasive speaker that he sent even his enemies into ecstasies by arguing one side of a question and then, pausing only to mop his brow, arguing just as forcefully the other side. The Romans thought so highly of Prohaeresius that they built a 9-foot statue of him inscribed: "From Rome, the Queen of Cities, to the King of Eloquence." If this great respect for the ability to argue on either the true or false side of a question seems somewhat misplaced, we must remember that in our trial courts today a good lawyer is supposed to be able to argue equally well that (a) the culprit undoubtedly stole the diamond, and that (b) he was at home reading to his old mother at the time of the crime.

The Roman orator cared less than the Greek for arguing fine points of philosophy. His purpose was political—to sway the senate or the crowd with his speech. His art stood for more than tricky persuasion. Quintilian, an educator who lived during the first century A.D., summed up the Roman ideal of oratory: "Now according to my definition no man can be a complete orator unless he is a good man; I therefore require that he should not only be accomplished in eloquence, but possessed of every moral virtue. . . . For I account no one to be an orator if he is not an honest man."

At the school of the rhetor, the youth learned not only to orate but to think and reason clearly, to see both sides of a question, and to present his conclusions, backed up by his knowledge of the law, in the best possible language.

Thus the little Roman boy, if he had the good fortune to be born a citizen and if his father could afford his education, grew up to take his stately place in the government of the vast Roman Empire.

MEDIEVAL TIMES

In European history, the years between A.D. 500 and 1000 are generally called the Dark Ages. They were years darkened by warfare and destruction; by ignorance, greed, and cruelty; by all the forces that crush a civilization rather than propel it forward.

The vast and glorious Roman Empire had toppled—a prey, perhaps, to its own greed, and certainly to the onslaughts of barbarian hordes swarming down from the north. These various tribes battled with each other as well as with the peoples whom they wished to conquer. Primitive and illiterate, they cared more for power and plunder than for arts and learning. During these dark waves of violence, the flame of knowledge flickered very low.

Meanwhile, the Christian religion had become firmly established. The gentle teachings of the young Jew, Jesus Christ, had started quietly enough in Judea, a small outpost of the Roman Empire. But his followers had spread his words of hope and comfort to neighboring countries, even to Rome itself. The new religion taught belief in the brotherhood of man, the forgiveness of sin by a loving God, and the promise of a better life after death. Such a faith, like water to the thirsty, brought hope to the oppressed, war-weary common peoples of the empire.

At first the Roman rulers had outlawed this religion as unpatriotic and blasphemous toward their old gods. But the faith continued to spread and take on more converts until, in the year 311, the emperor Galerius passed a law permitting the Christians to worship as they chose.

Soon Christianity became the official religion of Rome. The efficient Romans organized the simple faith of Jesus Christ into a system of pope, bishops, priests, abbots and abbesses, monks and nuns, with a ritual of worship and a glory of cathedrals and churches and music and holy accouterments that outshone the drama of their old pagan festivals. Thus Christianity, with all the highest arts of mankind newly dedicated to the worship of God, spread like a dawn throughout the continent.

But the rules of the new faith, as set up by the Roman Catholic Church, worked against the pursuit of learning. In its efforts to force all people to conform strictly to its beliefs, the church forbade the study of the older "pagan" writers and thinkers, those who had made discoveries in science and in other areas before Christian times. Thus the church outlawed all the careful studies of Aristotle, Plato, Galen (the Greek physician), Euclid (the father of geometry), Ptolemy (the astronomer), and all the other scholars who had toiled toward knowledge at the universities of Athens and Alexandria. All such studies were now forbidden. In the year 401 Saint Augustine, the great Christian father, forbade the clergy even to read the books of pre-Christian writers; and in 529 the emperor Justinian ordered the closing of all non-Christian schools and universities. Only the "pagan" Mohammedans (and some scholarly monks in Britain who were too far from Rome to know any better) kept alive the works of the old scholars, preserving them for posterity.

Thus, during the early Middle Ages, knowledge not only failed to advance in Europe, but was set back by hundreds of years. It was as if today's children not only did not have to go to school, but were commanded to forget everything they had ever learned. Only in the monasteries, the chill dwelling places of groups of devout Christian men who had withdrawn from the pleasures of life the better to worship and serve God, were the arts of reading and writing still carried on.

For the writings of the early Christian fathers and the words of the church services had to be made available to the growing numbers of churches and monasteries. Since there was no printing, the manuscripts had to be copied by hand. The work was done by "writing monks," members of a monastery who at least knew how to hold a pen and copy words onto parchment. Had it not been for the patient work of these monks who copied and recopied the sacred manuscripts, the knowledge of reading and writing would have been lost entirely to Europe.

Indeed, to tell the truth, many of the writing monks were not very good at it themselves. The writings, of course, were all in Latin; and from the numbers of mistakes in surviving copies, it is obvious that many of the good brothers did not even understand what they were writing down.

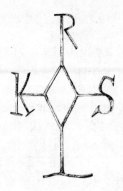

The Palace School

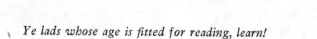

Ye lads whose age is fitted for reading, learn!
—Alcuin

Charlemagne, king of the Franks, was an exception among the ruthless, plundering Teutonic "barbarians." He admired the civilization of the Romans. He did his best to plant this civilization throughout his own realms, which included what is now France, Belgium, Holland, Switzerland, parts of western Germany, northern Italy, and northern Spain. He was an ardent Christian and a fine figure of a man—6 feet 4 inches in height— and a little vain about his looks. His daily dress was the rough homespun Frankish tunic of his people, but for state occasions he liked to dress in Roman robes embroidered with gold, a jeweled girdle, and a dazzling crown. But even more than their beautiful clothes, he admired the Romans' culture and their Latin tongue, which was the language of the church as well as of Greco-Roman literature. From his palace at Aachen, in that part of Europe which was later to become Germany, he sent to York in England to invite a monk named Alcuin to come and live with him and to be his minister of education. Alcuin was to begin his duties by teaching Charlemagne and his family to read and write Latin. The monk accepted.

Alcuin was a lovable fellow. Of himself, he told the story that as a young student, an *oblate*, living in a monastery and dedicated to holy orders, he had been lazy. We might not agree as to his laziness; his schedule of prayers, work, and study left him little more time for sleep than a soldier at the battlefront. After assisting at evening and midnight services in the chapel, he was expected to wake at cockcrow to sing at the matins service. There were no alarm clocks to awaken him, nothing but the monastery bell, which rang so often day and night that Alcuin and his cellmate—another lazy one—often slept through its clanging. One morning, with the noise of the bell still fading in his ears, Alcuin awoke to find the little cell full of direful demons engaged in beating and pummeling his room-mate. At his startled cry the demons turned and noticed Alcuin. As they advanced to start working on him he leapt from bed, crossed himself, and sang a psalm at the top of his lungs . . . at which point the demons, of course, disappeared, and Alcuin and his friend sped to the chapel, late but saved. He always vowed that he was grateful to his unholy visitors, for never again did he sleep through the bell for matins.

At Charlemagne's palace Alcuin still arose at dawn, for now he had to prepare the questions and answers that made up the day's lessons. It was good that he was an amiable fellow as well as an early riser, for the palace school was like no school before or since. It was attended by Charlemagne himself, his queen, his three sons, his two daughters, his son-in-law, and a number of priests and scholars of the kingdom. In addition to this gathering of the elite, there were also certain promising lads from the "town."

A medieval town was small, by our standards, but was as self-sufficient as a tiny nation. Surrounding its palace were its cathedral, its farms, its granaries, its vineyards, workrooms for weaving and dyeing materials, a tannery, ironworks, a black-smith's shop, a cooper's shop, and a woodworking shop. In short, almost everything that was used by its people was made within the limits of the little town. It was from among the sons of laborers and artisans that the boys were chosen to take lessons with the king and his family.

The lessons, of course, were in Latin. And the Latin had to be fluent and accurate. For Charlemagne—the mighty king and warrior whose sports were hunting and warfare, who was said to have slain 4,500 Saxon prisoners at one slaughter, and who was later to be crowned emperor of the West—Charlemagne was a great stickler for Latin grammar. He dreamed of a kingdom in which all his subjects would be both godly and good at Latin. He walked among the bent heads of the chosen boys, scolding those who wasted time, urging all to harder study.

Alcuin did his best with his ill-assorted pupils. He could not teach Greek, which Charlemagne would have liked to learn; or astronomy, another ambition of the monarch. But he taught his students what he knew, collected books from monasteries for them to study, and even wrote some textbooks himself.

And now books were no longer of paper or parchment. They were made in codex form—that is, folded sheets of vellum (the treated skin of an animal), stitched together and bound between hard covers. Since they were all handwritten they were still scarce, so that the library Alcuin collected for his pupils was a precious gift. He taught them to read and respect books—particularly the younger lads, whom he perhaps found easier to teach than the older members of the court.

He urged: "The years go by like running water. Waste not the teachable days in idleness! The flowing wave returns not, and the hastening hour returns not."

Their reading matter was the work of early Christian writers untainted by the ideas of the earlier pagan scholars. When it came to science, however, or indeed any factual knowledge, Alcuin had to write the textbook himself. Prince Pepin, the middle son of Charlemagne, was Alcuin's favorite pupil. At sixteen this lad probably was more interested in facts than in religious views; it was to him that Alcuin dedicated his text-

book entitled *Disputation of Pepin, the Most Noble and Royal Youth, with Albinus the Scholastic.* "Albinus" was the nickname by which Alcuin preferred to be called. His *Disputation*, composed of a long series of questions and answers, as was the fashion with textbooks, gives us an idea of the lessons with which the good monk busied himself at dawn:

PEPIN: What is the head?
ALBINUS: The top of the body.
PEPIN: What is the body?
ALBINUS: The domicile of the soul.
PEPIN: What is speech?
ALBINUS: The interpreter of the soul.
PEPIN: What makes speech?
ALBINUS: The tongue.
PEPIN: What is the tongue?
ALBINUS: The whip of the air.

This fascinating dialogue, wandering on for pages, was all to be learned by heart. If it seems rather ridiculous for a bright boy of sixteen to bother with, remember that it was all in Latin, and Pepin's native tongue was German. Perhaps to memorize these pages was as good a way as any of learning Latin.

As the *Disputation* goes on to the natural sciences, it becomes quite lyrical:

PEPIN: What is the sun?
ALBINUS: The splendor of the universe, the beauty of the sky.
PEPIN: What is the moon?
ALBINUS: The eye of the night, the dispenser of dew, the prophet of the storms.
PEPIN: What are the stars?
ALBINUS: The pictures of the roof of the heavens, the guides of sailors, the ornaments of night. . . .

—and so on, through pages of "facts" that would make a modern six-year-old laugh. One of the most delightful scientific definitions of all time is:

PEPIN: What is snow?
ALBINUS: Dry water.

The palace school pupils also learned to write, using the new Caroline miniscule script named for Charlemagne himself. This writing was such an improvement over the old run-the-words-together method that it spread to all copyists and schools throughout Europe. For the first time, capital letters were used at the beginning of sentences, spaces were left between words, and punctuation was used within and after sentences. One can see, by comparing them, how much easier to read was this script than the old Roman. It was also easier to copy. Whatever else Charlemagne's school accomplished, it gave the world the means of making clean, legible manuscripts which laid the foundation for later printing.

Alcuin's pupils practiced forming these letters on wax tablets which, like those of the Romans, could be smoothed over and used again and again. Charlemagne himself, alas, never mastered the craft of writing. He tried hard, keeping his tablets under the pillows of his couch for practice at odd moments; but he never became easy in it. He had started late in life, and his great hands were used to managing horses and spears; even Alcuin could not tame them to form the small, neat letters. It is doubtful, however, that Alcuin scolded him.

Palace school students even learned a little arithmetic. Enough, perhaps, to enable a noble or an artisan to manage his own affairs. For this subject Alcium wrote another textbook containing problems such as this: "After a farmer has turned three times at each end of the field, how many furrows has he plowed?"

For exercise, Charlemagne's own sons were taught riding, hunting, the arts of war, and swimming in the delicious, warm springs of Aachen. Certainly the sons of nobles joined them in these sports, and perhaps some of the young town scholars. For Charlemagne, like the Chinese emperors of old, chose his officials from the graduates of his school, and he would have insisted that they be vigorous as well as bookish.

As the king himself progressed in Latin, he became distressed by the ignorance of the clergy throughout his realm. He dictated a letter to the abbot of Fulda, a leading monastery in his kingdom, complaining that "We have frequently received letters from monks and in them we recognize correct sentiments, but an uncouth style and language." He therefore ordered all bishops in his realm to provide free schools for all children, from whatever walk of life, who would like to attend. One of his orders, dated 789, directs that "every monastery and every abbey have its school, where boys may be taught the Psalms, the system of musical notation, singing, arithmetic, and grammar; and let books which are given them be free from faults, and let care be taken that the boys do not spoil them, either when reading or writing."

The great Frankish ruler who had conquered and slaughtered so many thousands of human beings would allow no blots or finger marks on the pages of a book! For books, in those dark days, were more precious than human lives.

The bishops obeyed their king as best they could. Theodulf, bishop of Orléans, ordered his diocese: "Let the priests hold schools in their towns and villages, and if any of the faithful wish to entrust their children to them for the learning of letters, let them not refuse. . . . Moreover, let them teach them from pure affection, remembering that it is written, 'The wise shall shine as the splendor of the firmament.' "

And so there sprang up a wide scattering of church schools where boys, although they might not always shine with quite such splendor, could learn at least to sing psalms, scratch Latin words on wax tablets, and count the furrows plowed by that toiling farmer. Indeed, for a few years there was quite a flurry of elementary schools for such studies in Europe.

But more barbarians came to conquer. Charlemagne's empire was shattered and his teachers scattered, and the flame of learning sank again to embers.

The Church Takes Over

*His aim is to improve the soul, not to teach, and to
train up to a virtuous, not an intellectual life.*

—JUSTIN MARTYR

Throughout Europe during the Middle Ages, as in ancient
Egypt and India, all schooling was in the hands of holy men.
Only in cathedrals, churches, and monasteries could a lad find
instruction in simple reading and writing. Indeed, the only
books to be had were those made in monasteries.

As we have seen at the palace school, Christian books were
no longer written on rolls or scrolls but on pages bound together in the form that books take today. Compared to modern
books they were cumbersome, difficult to read, and very beautiful.

With neither paper mills nor printing presses, the making of
each book was a complicated affair. Monks prepared parchment pages from skins of animals. They soaked these skins in
limewater to loosen the hair, then scraped them clean with a

wide tool made of bone. The skins were stretched on frames to dry and were then scraped again and again until they were thin and pliable. These parchment sheets were then folded twice into squares, each sheet forming two double pages. They were trimmed to size, stitched together, and bound between wooden boards covered with pigskin to form a volume.

In the *scriptorium*, or writing room of the monastery, the good monks then filled these pages with their neat Caroline writing. Sometimes one monk would copy a whole book; sometimes a number of monks worked together, writing down what the abbot would dictate to them—a timesaving method that often made for interesting variations in spelling. The black or red ink used for the writing was also made by the monks, as were the other colored inks used to decorate the borders of pages. These decorations, called "illuminations," were lovely and intricate designs of flowers, fruits, small beasties, and curlicues, all painted in jewellike colors.

So precious were these handmade volumes that the monastery kept them chained with stout brass to the racks of its library. And if some villain were bold enough to file through the chain while the monks were at prayer, he might be sure of punishment in the next world. Dire warnings such as this were written on the flyleaves of books:

> This book belongs to Saint Maximin at his monastery of Micy, which abbot Peter caused to be written and with his own labor corrected and punctuated, and on Holy Thursday dedicated to God and Saint Maximin on the altar . . . with this imprecation, That he who should take it away from thence should incur damnation with the traitor Judas, with Annas, Caiaphas, and Pilate. Amen.

All the books, of course, were religious works: the gospels, the church services, the writings of Christian fathers. Few people ever saw them, let alone read them. The Middle Ages, with their feudal system of nobles, clergy, peasants, and serfs, were certainly not democratic. There was a strong feeling among the

upper classes that it was wrong for people to try to better themselves; that they should be content to remain in the state of ignorance and humility in which God had placed them. One abbot even imposed a fine on any peasants whom he found sending their children to priests for lessons! And many people agreed with Saint Ambrose, a fourth-century bishop, who declared that slaves were particularly fortunate in having the blessed opportunity to practice humility and to love their enemies! Thus, for the most part, people of the peasant, villein (tenant farmer), and serf classes were born, toiled, and died ignorant and dirty. Undoubtedly they managed to have some pleasure in their lives: dancing, games, and merry songs—all pastimes forbidden by the church. Some of the young "clerks" may even have envied them, particularly in warm weather—at least they worked outdoors, instead of in a stuffy cell.

But as the church grew, in both area and power, it needed more men who could read and write to carry on its organization. In 826 the church council at Rome decreed, as had Charlemagne before it, that "bishops should appoint masters able to teach the liberal arts and the articles of faith in all dioceses and parishes." Thus teaching became not only a sideline but the legal responsibility of the church; and a good many promising small boys started going to school.

SONG SCHOOL

A boy of eight or nine, if he was poor, lucky, and had a good singing voice, might be invited to attend song school. Such a school, attached to a church or cathedral, trained choir boys to sing at Mass. In return for their services as choristers they were given sleeping space, board, and lessons in reading and writing elementary Latin—at least enough to know what they were chanting. They were expected to sweep out the church, fetch and carry for the priests, and do any other chores to assist their elders and betters.

The little boys worked hard for few comforts. Their quarters were crowded; often they slept two or three in a bed. But they must have been tired enough to sleep standing up—and no doubt often did. For after singing the evening services of Vespers and Compline, and retiring to huddled beds, they were awakened again at midnight to sing Nocturnes in the cold, dark church. Throughout the night they had to be on hand to pipe the services: Lauds, Prime, the Seven Psalms with the litanies, the first Mass, Tierce, and another Mass at daylight; then Sext; then breakfast and a nap; and awakened again for Nones; after which they yawned their way through a few hours of lessons in psalms and Latin letters, and were at last sent to play—with a stern warning not to be late for evening service!

When a boy had finished elementary song-school, if he showed promise and his family could spare him from work at home, he could go on to study at the nearest monastery or church or cathedral. These schools were all very much alike; but life at the monastery was perhaps the most varied and interesting, and so we shall look at such a school.

MONASTIC SCHOOL

The medieval monastery was a small self-supporting world of its own. Between prayer and religious services, the monks labored in the fields, growing vegetables and fruits; or in the storage cellars, putting down fine wines and cheeses; or, as we have shown, in the scriptorium, copying books by hand. By the tenth century the monasteries also went in for teaching, accepting not only *oblati*, boys studying for the priesthood, but a number of *externi*, or outsiders who wished to learn. These boys started school at about the age of ten and kept at it until they were eighteen. Their parents paid a small fee for their board and keep. They were housed in a dormitory outside the monastic walls. They did not have to join in as many religious observances as the student-priests, but otherwise their life and classes were the same.

The pupil's first lesson was in manners. The rules required him to "kneel when answering the Abbot, not to take his seat unbidden, not to loll against the wall nor fidget with things

within reach. He is not to scratch himself, nor cross his legs like a tailor. He is to wash his hands before meals, keep his knife sharp and clean, not to seize upon vegetables, and not to use his spoon in the common dish."

During classes the boys sat in rows on low stools or on clean straw on the floor. The oblati sat together in one group, the externi in another.

The lessons, of course, were all in Latin. The boys had to speak in Latin, and their grammar, as Charlemagne urged, had to be correct. They were drilled in questions and answers that had to be learned by heart, such as:

BOYS: Master, we children ask you to teach us to speak correctly, for we are unlearned and speak corruptly.

MASTER: What do you want to say?

BOYS: What do we care what we say so long as we speak correctly and say what is useful, not old-womanish or improper.

MASTER: Are you willing to be flogged while learning?

BOYS: We would rather be flogged while learning than remain ignorant; but we know that you will be kind to us, and not flog us unless you are obliged to . . .

In this pious frame of mind, the boys went on to tackle those subjects prescribed for study in the Middle Ages, which were known as the "seven liberal arts." Actually they were not at all liberal and, except for music, had little to do with the arts. They were divided into two sets of courses: the first three, or the *trivium*, were grammar, rhetoric, and a subject called "dialectic" (or logic); the second group, the *quadrivium*, were arithmetic, geometry, astronomy, and music. While all these subjects were based on the works of pre-Christian Greek and Roman scholars, they had been diluted and altered by church authorities to conform to the current religious principles. And thus they were taught to struggling scholars for many hundreds of years.

A Roman grammarian, Aelius Donatus, had written a grammar textbook for children in the fourth century. It was one of the few books without decorations of any kind. Perhaps this made it seem important and solemn enough to be harmless; at any rate, Donatus was the standard text on grammar for centuries. His was a dreary book, teaching its rules in a sort of catechism:

> How many parts of speech are there?—Eight.
> What are they?—Noun, pronoun, adjective, adverb, participle, conjunction, preposition, and interjection.
> What is a noun?—A part of speech with case, signifying a body or thing particularly or commonly.
> How many attributes have nouns?—Six.
> What are they?—Quality, comparison, gender, number, figure, and case.

Some of the pagan classics were allowed for the study of grammar. Although Alcuin himself had sternly warned against the poetry of Vergil—"The sacred poets are sufficient for you; there is no reason why you should sully your mind with the rank luxuriance of Vergil's verse . . ."—schoolboys could now dissect the poet into his grammatical parts. The singing first line of the *Aeneid*, which Roman boys had chanted with joy, was treated thus:

> What part of speech is *arma?*—A noun.
> Of what sort?—Common.
> Of what class?—Abstract.
> Of what gender?—Neuter.
> Why neuter?—Because all nouns whose plural end in *a* are neuter.[!]

If the boys managed to keep awake after repeated doses of this kind of thing, they went on to rhetoric.

This was no longer the art of making fine speeches, as in the heyday of Greece and Rome. It was more like composition. It not only covered the reading of church history and the study of church writers, but it also covered the composition of letters and even of legal documents—an art that, up to this time, could only be performed by monks and clergymen.

Dialectic was the high-sounding name for logic, or reasoning. and though "faith" and "reason" posed questions that were being argued by a number of thinkers at the time, it is certain that boys in a monastic school were not encouraged to question the reasoning of their teachers.

When they had covered these three subjects, the young scholars went on to their quadrivium. But now, even more than in the trivium, the teaching was colored by religion. And the efforts of the holy authorities to bring religion into a subject like arithmetic were sometimes amusing.

The science of numbers had not progressed very far in Europe. It was considered part of the pagan knowledge of the Greeks and Saracens and was frowned upon as tainted with black magic. Although Arabic numerals were already in use in pagan countries, the clergy refused to teach these diabolical symbols that were used by pagans to measure unknown mysteries. However, arithmetic was useful, even to Christians. A great teacher named Rabanus Maurus, who had been a pupil of Alcuin, decided that a certain amount of it could safely be taught without endangering the boys' souls. "In the gospel," he explained, "the Saviour says, 'The very hairs of your head are numbered' "—which proved that counting was not immoral!

The boys were taught some interesting things about the properties of numbers. The number 4, for instance, had a "certain perfection of solidarity" because its parts—1, 2, 3, and 4—all added up to 10, which is not only the number of a man's fingers, but also the number of years in a decade! and therefore a very important number. This number had other admirable qualities: there were 4 seasons, 4 virtues, 4 vices, and 4 ages of man. And by multiplying these two excellent numbers—4 and 10—one arrived at 40, which proved that 40 was, without a doubt, the correct number of days for Lenten fasting!

The clumsy Roman numerals still in use in Christian schools did not tempt further interest in mathematics. But toward the end of the tenth century an ingenious priest named Gerbert (who afterward became Pope Sylvester II) figured out a way of listing these numerals in columns according to multiples of 10 and "carrying" into the next column, as we do today. A comparison of a sum as the Romans wrote it, as Gerbert wrote it, and as we write it today shows how he bridged the gap between Roman math and modern math.

Roman	Gerbert				Arabic
	(M	C	X	I)	
MCIIV	I	II		IV	1,204
DXXXVIII		V	III	VIII	538
MMCCCCLV	II	IV	V	V	2,455
DCXIX		VI	I	IX	619
MMMMDCCCXVI	IV	VIII	I	VI	4,816

But while many schoolboys and their teachers must have blessed Gerbert for simplifying arithmetic by putting multiples of ten into separate columns, there were still some church authorities who, because he had studied in Spain where the pagan Saracens were teaching, accused him of consorting with the Devil and would have none of his ideas.

"Geometry" was perhaps the most fascinating subject of all. It had nothing to do with geometry before or since; the work of Euclid, the Greek geometrist, had been destroyed by Christian zealots. The geometry of the Middle Ages was a sort of fairy-tale geography, which resulted in some startling maps drawn by means of guesswork and a bulk of misinformation about peoples, plants, and animals. This lore had been gathered from ancient and very imaginative Roman writers and embroidered by hearsay. Thus the schoolboy learned some fearsome "facts."

The seas, he was taught, were inhabited by sirens who beguiled poor seamen to their death with their sweet singing. It was in this way that the Devil seized all sinners who lent an ear to sweet music and pretty voices. Monkeys had no tails (*cauda*) because they were creatures of the Devil, and the Devil had no Holy Scripture (*caudex*). Lionesses gave birth to lifeless cubs that did not breathe for three days, until their father (representing God) came and breathed life into them.

They also learned of fabulous salamanders and phoenixes which performed miraculous feats with fire, symbol of the flames of hell. The elephant and his wife, because they ate from trees, represented Adam and Eve; and the only creature which could overpower them was the serpent Satan in the form of a dragon. (This same dragon, variously pictured according to the artist's own nightmare, could be overcome by the sweet-smelling belch of a tiger—who represented the Church of Christ.) And the hypocritical crocodile, while pretending to live "holily and justly by day," at night indulged himself by lolling luxuriously in the water.

Astronomy was another haphazard subject. While pagan countries had been progressing in the study of the planets and in the inventing of instruments for measuring the skies, little of this knowledge had reached Europe. It was by now generally accepted that the earth was round; but it was still fixed in space, with the other heavenly bodies revolving around it. Moreover, the subject of astronomy was confusingly mixed up with astrology, a pseudo science which contends that the planets control the lives of individual human beings. This kind of superstition appealed particularly to the Germanic barbarians, who had recently come from a world of thick forests peopled with mysterious spirits. The church tried to outlaw such beliefs as pagan and against the will of God. But some of the superstitions kept creeping into the sparse Christian knowledge of astronomy—for after all, did not the Scriptures tell of punishment by days of darkness, and of comets and thunderstorms bespeaking the wrath of God?

Most of the teaching monks, however, made no pretense of understanding the solar system. They preferred to agree with the early Christian writer Origen that while there was certainly "writing in the stars," only the angels could read it. And it was safer to leave these things to the angels.

Music, the fourth subject of the quadrivium, meant the study of church music. Its theory—the mathematical division of the octave—was known to the Middle Ages through Boethius, a sixth-century Roman scholar, who in turn learned it from those natural musicians, the Greeks. Boys in monastic schools had to learn music and harmony and had to lift up their voices in plainsong. The chants were beautiful, and no doubt the boys enjoyed this one outlet for their spirits—for no games or sports were allowed at school. Even the clergy appears to have become overenthusiastic about singing. Pope Gregory the Great, who brought together and systematized the entire body of liturgical chant, chided that "at divine service, more is thought of a good voice than of a good life. Consequently no deacon may, henceforth, sing in the church except the gospel and the mass."

A monastic schoolboy worked hard. His lessons were stiff and often as dry as straw; his bed was hard and his sleep short. Discipline was severe. The good monks had been taught that the body was the enemy of the soul and were glad to punish it. Like the Romans and the Hebrews before them, they did not spare the rod. At a certain German monastery, all the students were whipped regularly once a month, just to be on the safe side. And at Glastonbury Abbey, in England, the boys were all flogged on Christmas Eve—to make the holiday sweeter.

But historical accounts tend to leave out the fun and laughter that is bound to have been a part of school life, even in a monastery. The monks, after all, were gentle and sympathetic souls, teaching "from affection." And there was one day of the year when even the strictest monastery or cathedral school grew hilarious. This was on Childermas, or Holy Innocents' Day, which falls on the twenty-eighth of December. On that day the boys were allowed to change places with the masters—to run the school as they wished, to give out the lessons to their teachers, and to award black marks and punishment—and, at the end of the day, forgiveness.

GIRLS' SCHOOLING

Nothing has been said about the education of girls during the Middle Ages. There was very little of it. There were convents for nuns, it is true, which often took in young girls and taught them beautiful lettering and how to paint manuscripts, and trained them to do exquisite embroidery on altar cloths and other church draperies. But most girls were simply taught at home according to the principles of Saint Jerome: "To spin wool, to hold the distaff, to put the basket in her lap, to turn the spinning wheel and to shape the yarn with her thumb."

Girls of noble birth, however, were often given private lessons by tutors in their fathers' castles. Besides manners and morals, they might learn to read and write in both Latin and French; and to sing, embroider, manage a household, and make herb poultices to soothe the wounds of knights.

Of this kind of life, so different from life in a monastery, we shall learn by taking a look at chivalry and its training of knights.

The School of Chivalry

He was a verray, parfit, gentil knyght.

—CHAUCER

The word *chivalry* comes from the same Frankish word as *cavalry* and originally meant horsemanship. Today, when we speak of someone as chivalrous we do not mean that he is a good horseman; we mean that he is particularly polite toward the ladies. How did the word for management of horses come to mean charming manners?

After the death of Charlemagne, the lands of Europe fell into the hands of a great number of nobles. Some of them were princes, descendants of former kings; some were leaders of those conquering "barbarian" tribes from the north and east. The various domains of these nobles were like small kingdoms, each ruled according to the feudal system. A reigning noble was served by a sort of standing army of knights who lived rather grandly in manor houses or even fortresses in return for their promise to do battle for their overlord. Under the protection of the knights were the common people: the artisans who produced the necessary goods for living, the workmen, the servants, and the serfs who labored in the fields and who, like the crops they raised, belonged to the land.

The nobles were in constant competition with each other for more land, more power. All of Europe was engaged in these small feudal wars. The common people could only survive through the protection of their nobles; the nobles, in turn, could only survive through their military strength. And military strength, in those days, meant horsemen—armed, helmeted, and full of courage. It was the training of youths to become such horsemen that gave rise to the way of life called chivalry.

It was through the church that chivalry became something more than horsemanship. The barbarian leaders, even though they were now willingly joining the church, were rough and boorish. And although the church could not turn them into bookworms, it did its best to gentle them by teaching a code of honor, loyalty, good manners, and respect for God and their betters. The lords responded; they needed the good will of the clergy, and they undoubtedly enjoyed being elegant and admirable. They consented to pursue their battlesome careers according to honorable standards, and to bring up their sons by those standards. And thus chivalry became a world of knights and ladies, coats of arms and horses, gauntlets and battles, and ladies' handkerchiefs and roses.

This world of chivalry, it must be remembered, was limited to the ruling classes. But it flourished for a good three hundred years, and it has left its mark in story, song, and history. And while its youth did not actually go to school, as such, their training was so organized and special that it must be included in any story of schools. Besides, it is fun to read about.

A boy began his training for knighthood at the age of seven. Up to that age he had played at home with his family and nurse; but now he was sent to live in the manor or castle of one of his father's friends—perhaps his overlord, perhaps another knight, perhaps a wealthy bishop. There, with no whimpering and no parents to coddle him, he was to learn to serve his elders and to become a gentleman.

Instead of the "seven liberal arts," this boy learned the "seven perfections": riding, swimming, archery, fencing, hunting, chess, and rhyming.

He did not undertake all these subjects at once. For the first years of his training, he was taught by the lady of the castle. She taught him to be a good boy, to say his prayers, and to serve as her little page. He must come when called, bow from the waist, and remember where she had left her embroidery or her scent bottle. If she happened to be fond of music—and most ladies were—she taught him to sing and to dance. If she was a kind and playful lady, she had a good time with her little page and undoubtedly gave him as many candies, cuffs, and kisses as she gave her own children. Or, if she was the haughty sort and bored by children, she had ladies in waiting only too willing to amuse themselves by teaching a little boy how to behave.

Sometimes the lad was even given some lessons in reading and writing—not in Latin, but in the vernacular, the spoken language of whatever country he was in. But much book learning was considered sissyish by most of the gentry, who could neither read nor write themselves.

More important was his physical education. As a little fellow he was trained by an athletic teacher, or even by the lord of the manor himself, to run fast, to jump, to box and wrestle, to swim, to ride—and to love his horse. Compared to the boy in a monastery, he had a good time. And if he was ever homesick, there were plenty of loving ladies and games and sports to help him recover.

At the age of twelve the boy began his service to his lord. He still served the ladies; indeed, he was to serve them all his life, in true chivalrous fashion. But now he was allowed to help his master as a sort of young valet: to tend his clothes, polish his armor, pour his wine, and wait upon him at table. He did not feel that these were menial duties; rather they were masculine privileges, proving that he was a child no longer.

The School of Chivalry

It was at this age that he began to play chess. This game, said to have come from India, was a great favorite in manors and castles. Its very pieces—kings and queens, rooks (castles) and bishops, knights and pawns (foot soldiers)—speak of medieval times. It was not an easy game; and the young boy, who had not had schooling to train his mind, needed all his wits to play it passably.

At fourteen, if all went well, he became squire to his lord. And this role of squire (meaning shield-bearer) was indeed a manly one. It lasted for seven years of increasing duties. The lad now spent less time with the ladies and more time in the stables, grooming and training the horses, and tending the hunting hounds and the hawks that were used in the popular sport of falconry. When the knight rode forth, his young squire rode beside him to carry his shield, to hold his horse when he dismounted, even (if he was mature enough) to accompany him into battle.

The squire's physical training became more strenuous. He was now preparing in earnest for the noble art of warfare. Like the Greek boys before him, he had to run, leap, and scale walls while dressed in armor—but armor far more cumbersome than that of the Greeks. Indeed, he was so trussed up in chain mail and metal plate that it is a wonder he could move at all.

He was already a good horseman; now he had to learn how to use the weapons of war. These were the lance, the mace (a heavy spiked staff intended to shatter his enemy's armor), the battle-ax and sword for cutting off heads, and the dagger for closer work upon the fallen foe. His exercises with these weapons were done on horseback. Managing a spirited charger with one mailed hand, he whacked at a wooden post with his sword as he dashed by, or reached with his lance to spear a ring in passing.

His greatest challenge was tilting at the *quintain*. This was a swiveling post with a crosspiece nailed to it, a target in its center. If the charging horseman hit the center of the target, well and good; he merely broke his lance and scored a direct hit. But if his lance struck off-center, the crosspiece whirled around to crack him on the back of the head as he passed. Because of his stout helmet this blow did not kill him, but it usually knocked him ignominiously from his horse.

Such skills prepared the youth not only for war against his lord's enemies, but for that mock warfare that was the high sport of the day—the tournament. This contest of knighthood was as admired as is baseball in our country today or cricket in England. One tournament event, jousting, amounted to a sort of fencing on horseback. With the riders all encased in their chain underwear and metal suits, it was an awkward game—far from the agile riding and swift movement of polo. But the point of the game, as in polo, was accuracy. The knights of the opposing teams rode at each other, their armor and that of their horses clanking and jingling. The aim was either to break one's lance against an opponent's armor or to unseat him from his horse. The victor was awarded trophies, glory, and the loving looks of the ladies, who were an enthusiastic audience at these affairs.

His day's exercises over, the young squire went on to his duties in the manor hall. He attended the knightly dinner, carving the roasted meat for his lord, carrying on sprightly conversation with the ladies. After the meal he was encouraged to dance, to sing, to sigh lovingly, and to recite pretty rhymes composed for this lady or that. He could never be forward— that would have been considered low-class and oafish—and he had to be at all times polite and attentive, even after a hard day's hunting or fighting.

The life agreed with him. The poet Chaucer wrote of a typical young squire:

> Singing he was, or fluting all the day;
> He was as fresh as is the month of May . . .
> Short was his gown, with sleeves long and wide.
> Well could he sit on horse, and fairly ride . . .
> Courteous he was, humble and serviceable,
> And carved before his father at the table.

94

The School of Chivalry

When a youth reached the age of twenty, he had to choose a lady as the object of his devotion. She was to be his ideal of womanhood, one to whom he would always be faithful in spirit, whose interests he would always serve, and to whom he dedicated his love poems. The choice was not a very serious one. He was not going to marry this lady; and indeed she was often married already. Frequently she was the same lady who had wiped his tears and tossed a ball for him when he was her little page. She was merely a lady to whom he dedicated his allegiance for the rest of his life. Whether he continued to serve her after he found a wife is another story. But at any rate, this ideal devotion was probably good training toward making a good husband.

At twenty-one the squire was ready for knighthood—that is, if he had behaved well, had done well in his activities, and generally proved himself a worthy candidate for that honor. Had he slouched at his duties, or been poor at horsemanship or rude or uncouth toward his betters, he was merely sent home as a "dropout." But if his youthful service had been satisfactory, he would now become a full-fledged defender of the land.

The ceremony of knighthood was a serious occasion. The young candidate was given several weeks of intense religious instruction. His responsibilities toward God, his country, and his fellow men were carefully gone over. On the eve of the great day he was bathed, then dressed in a white garment and black hose. All night he knelt before the church altar, praying that he might be worthy of this honor.

With the dawn came the priest bearing the Holy Sacrament. Then followed a ceremony as solemn and as joyful as a wedding, with clergy and knights and ladies in attendance. Handing his sword to the priest, the youth swore an oath not unlike that of the Greek epheboi: "to defend the church, to attack the wicked, to respect the priesthood, to protect women and the poor, to preserve the country in tranquility, and to shed [his] blood in behalf of [his] brethren."

The School of Chivalry

The priest blessed the sword at the altar and returned it to the youth, exhorting him to live up to his oath. And now the master—the knight whom he had been serving since childhood —drew his own sword, laid its flat tip on the shoulder of the kneeling youth, and pronounced the solemn words: "In the name of God and of our Lady, and the patron saint, and of Saint Michael and Saint George, I dub thee knight. Be brave, bold, and loyal."

The young knight arose. The ladies decked him in his new equipment: his armor, his golden chain, his sword belt and his sword—all symbols of his new estate. A fine feast was held in his honor, with dancing, songs, and the wine flowing free.

And now our young knight was free to marry, to take up life in a fine manor provided by his lord, and to take other little boys into his home for their training for knighthood.

The Universities

Gaudeamus igitur
Juvenes dum sumus . . .

—a song of the wandering scholars

Knowledge, like sunlight, cannot be kept secret. Even during the so-called Dark Ages in Europe there were thinking men whose minds, while loyal to the rulings of their church, were hungry for more learning. Some of them had gotten hold of the ancient classics by one means or another and had pondered them.

But it was those restless knights of chivalry who accidentally opened the windows of Europe to let in the light of knowledge. In the eleventh, twelfth, and thirteenth centuries they set forth on their Crusades to conquer the infidels living in the East and the Holy Land. When they reached these countries, they found that the Moslem inhabitants not only enjoyed greater luxuries of silks, arts, and pleasant foods than they themselves had ever known, but knew far more than even the most scholarly teachers in cathedrals and monasteries at home.

And how had the Moslems become so learned? A simple Arabian race with no education of their own, they had swarmed over those parts of the ancient Greek and Roman empires that had not become part of Christendom. But they were a quick-minded people, ready to absorb the learning of those lands and to improve it with further studies. While Europe was still struggling with simple arithmetic, the Moslems had long been using the "Arabic" numerals 1, 2, 3, 4, 5, 6, 7, 8, 9, 0, and were applying them to problems in algebra, geometry, and even physics. It is said that the Arabs had gotten these numerals from the Hindus, together with a good deal of advanced mathematics, which they labored to define and improve.

Their religion did not forbid knowledge but rather encouraged it. They built libraries and schools, and high towers from which to chart the paths of the planets and the stars. They had discovered more about geography and navigation than Europe had dreamed of, and had made tremendous advances in science. They had invented a pendulum clock and a compass. They had discovered the refraction of light, atmospheric pressure, the law of gravity and capillary action. They had studied the soil and the sciences of fertilizers and even pesticides. They had compiled books on medicine. They had worked on alchemy in the hope of finding a way of turning other metals into gold; and although they never found the answer, they learned a good deal of chemistry in the process. And, even more tempting to the European knights and nobles, they had produced fine silks and tea, sugar and strawberries, spices and gunpowder.

As news of these wonders seeped into Europe, the scholars seized on the learning as eagerly as did the aristocrats on the luxuries. They translated; they compiled encyclopedias; they discussed. Some of the sciences that demanded reasoning instead of blind faith were hard for many of the clergy to swallow. But other great churchmen urged that there need be no war between fact and faith. So now, with the approval of the church itself, book learning became fashionable—indeed, more fashionable than it had ever been before in Europe. In the larger cities there sprang up centers of learning called "universities," places where scholars could meet with each other and with students seeking knowledge on one subject or another. And these centers of learning are the direct ancestors of our present-day universities.

The universities sprouting throughout Italy, France, Germany, England, Poland, and Spain specialized in different subjects: one was the place to go to study medicine, while others taught law, or theology, or philosophy, or the liberal arts. Students flocked from one country to another for the privilege of learning from a master in the field. Universities had no entrance requirements beyond an elementary knowledge of Latin and the ability to pay the fee. Students could enter at the age of fourteen, but many of them were oldsters in their thirties or forties.

Their lives were not easy. They lodged in whatever rooms they could rent in the town, assembling at dawn at the hall of learning—usually an unlit and unheated room in a building unwanted for any other use. Muffled in hats and cloaks against the drafty chill, they sat on the floor or, if they were lucky, on stiff wooden benches, and listened to the words of their master. With books still scarce and paper expensive, they took lecture notes on the old-fashioned wax tablets, only copying important knowledge into their precious personal notebooks which they compared and discussed with each other in the evenings and on weekends.

To make sure they got their money's worth, the pupils formed students' guilds which set up rules for the teacher. The latter, worthy soul, had to turn up on time for his classes, could not cut classes for any reason except serious illness (although he was allowed one day off for his honeymoon), had to speak distinctly and neither too quickly nor too slowly, and had to be sure to stick closely to the subject at hand—no wandering off on opinions of his own!

The young student's first four or five years were spent on the trivium—Latin grammar, rhetoric, and dialectic in Latin. When he could "define and determine"—that is, be fluent in Latin speech and its grammar—he was awarded a bachelor of arts degree. Another three or four years spent on the quadrivium—arithmetic, geometry, astronomy, and music—brought him his master's degree. After that, he might put in from eight to fourteen years before becoming a doctor in his special subject, at which time he was given a feast of celebration, a cap, a gown, and a diploma.

Although student life was rugged, it had its compensations. Students, for instance, were exempt from either taxes or military service. In this sense it was a carefree way of life, appealing to young men of all classes. Travel as well as learning had come into favor. The roads and the towns were soon filled with youths seeking knowledge—or perhaps just a good time. "Colleges" were set up for them; that is, living quarters with a master in charge to keep them in order.

Students with no money were permitted to beg on the streets for their tuition. Others had no need to beg; young nobles often brought their servants with them. One son of a Spanish grandee is said to have arrived at the University of Salamanca with a retinue consisting of a governor, a tutor, a cook, three valets, four lackeys, eight pages, and a long string of grooms for the horses! Other lads of wealth, more self-reliant, set out dressed as beggars in rags and tatters, with their tablets and styluses concealed in their knapsacks, to deceive the bandits lurking in the forests through which they must pass.

"Come one, come all" was the cry of the universities. And on horseback they came or on shanks' mare, from one country to another, to sample the lectures at the different founts of learning. Since the courses were all in Latin, language was no barrier. But there were jealousy and squabbles and sometimes bitter fighting between students of different nationalities. The "nations," as these groups were called, vied with each other not so much in scholarship as for the best seats in the classroom, the best housing, and general mischief.

So roisterous did they become that the universities had to set up strict rules of conduct. Some of these rules give us a lively picture of student life. Students were not only forbidden to steal or to climb into the college after its gates were shut, but they were not to forge their names, or wear daggers, or practice witchcraft. Nor might they frequent theaters or taverns, or keep dogs, monkeys, or bears in their rooms.

A student caught breaking such rules might be imprisoned, suspended, or—if, say, he persisted in keeping a bear in his room—expelled from the university.

A Boy with the Wandering Scholars

In the public house to die
Is my resolution . . .

—Goliard song

Without doubt, a number of young men attended the universities more for adventure than for reasons of scholarship. These wandering scholars, as they were called, begged and sang their way through an education of a sort, stopping where they could, paying what they could scrape up, but never taking seriously the rule against frequenting taverns. One group called themselves goliards. They claimed as their patron saint a quite mythical Bishop Golias, who was said to have greatly loved his food and drink. The happy-go-lucky goliards moved from town to town, singing for their suppers their catchy ditties:

> We in our wandering,
> Blithesome and squandering,
> Eat to satiety,
> Drink to propriety,
> Laugh till our sides we split,
> Rags on our bones to fit.
> Craft's in the bone of us;
> Fear is unknown to us . . .

The goliard songs, one must add, not only were gay but were composed in excellent Latin, so that the writers must have had not only wit and an ear for music but a good knowledge of the classical language.

As bright as these roving students may have been—and surely there were bright ones and dull ones, decent ones and no-goods—they all had to pay their fees for lodging and tuition. So they hit upon the idea of taking with them younger boys as servants, or "fags" as they were called in later English schools. These little fellows, sometimes only six or seven years old, waited upon their young masters, sang and begged for them in the streets, and even stole vegetables from the countryside. In return for such services they were promised big-brotherly care, a chance to see the world, and a fine education at a university—all for free.

So many little nippers were thus lured to the roads that many of the universities set up elementary schools for them. At these schools the little "A B C shooters," as they were called, could learn their letters and their "two times two"—all in Latin, of course—and so might themselves, in time, enter a university as qualified students. No provisions, however, were made for the bed and board of these children. While their teen-age masters slept in such lodgings as they could pay for, the little ones slept like puppies by the hearth in the schoolroom, or, in warm weather, on the sheltered, cushiony grass of graves in the churchyard. Their food was the leftovers of the bigger boys for whom they begged. And since beggars, when they roam the streets in great numbers, seldom get very rich, there was no money for clothes for the little fags. Hungry, half naked, and very far from home, they worked as less than slaves—as beggars—in the hope of an education.

This way of life, of course, did not befall the majority of small boys of the times. But it was prevalent enough to be a recognized form of schooling. And there is a contemporary account of the adventures of one such little fellow, a German boy named Hans Butzbach, who later became the abbot of a monastery.

Hans was one of many children born to a worthy weaver. At the age of five he was sent to the local parish school. He hated school and played hooky so often that one day his mother took him to the schoolmaster to ask that he be punished. But as she was going out the door she heard her little boy's screams and returned to find him bleeding from the lash. Horrified, she withdrew him from school. But what should she do with him next? If he would not learn how to read and write, what would his future be?

A neighbor's son, a stout lad of sixteen, had come home for his holidays from the university at Nürnberg. Eyeing Hans, now a healthy boy of ten, he offered to take him back to the university—that is, if the child's fond parents would put up the money for his books and clothing. The weaver and his wife were of course delighted at this opportunity for their problem child. Hans danced a jig of joy and ran to tell the neighbors that he'd be going away to become a scholar.

Next day Hans set forth with Master Willi. The first night they put up at an inn cheerful with firelight, the songs of traveling students, and the smell of roasting meat. But Willi, of course, had taken charge of Hans's money and was spending it on food and drink for himself and his friends, while Hans, too frightened to protest, curled up by the hearth to cry himself to sleep.

Morning came; strengthened by some bread and beer given to them by the innkeeper, the two set forth again for the University of Nürnberg. But when they reached that city, Willi espied some people from their home town who might recognize little Hans and carry home tales about the money. So he insisted that they travel farther in search of a better school. On and on they trudged, with the days spent in walking, and the evenings, for Hans, in begging—with a beating for reward if he did not collect a fat sum.

At last they were accepted at a school at Kadeň in Bohemia. Here Hans had his lessons in Latin letters by day, sang and begged in the streets at dusk, and at night cuddled up to the schoolroom stove. This life, though strenuous, was quite acceptable to Hans; after all, he was getting his education. He even learned to recite Donatus's Latin grammar by heart, even though he could not understand what it was all about. But Master Willi behaved so badly at this school that they were forced to leave.

At a town called Eger, Hans escaped from Willi and found a job as sort of pedagogue to a little boy of noble family, escorting him to and from school and generally keeping an eye on him. But Willi and his roistering friends caught up with Hans, whipped him for his desertion, and forced him back into their service.

From this time on the story of Hans, as told by himself after he had become an important churchman, becomes so adventurous that one wonders whether the abbot has not given in to the temptation of embroidering a good tale. But the story is there, from Abbot Hans's own pen; and should we not believe an abbot?

He writes that young Hans, now aged twelve, again ran away from the students and found a job as a waiter at an inn. Here he served so well that he was kidnaped by a wealthy Polish nobleman who needed a young squire. Hans, of course, had had no training in chivalry, could not ride a horse, swim, or manage a lance. He found himself being rented out as a sort of extra serving-boy to friends of his kidnaper—friends who, however, invariably returned him as unsatisfactory. Young Hans disliked this life. Not only was it boring to be rented out and returned like a horse, but he was getting no nearer his goal of learning to read Latin. Besides, his noble kidnaper was "low church"—less formal in its ritual than the Roman Catholic— which Hans found particularly distasteful. The kidnaper seems not to have found the arrangement very satisfactory either, for after two years (Hans was now old enough to enter a university, had he the requirements) his lord gave him outright to a Roman Catholic nobleman.

To this more sympathetic ear, Hans begged for his freedom. But his new master only thrashed him and took away his squire's livery until he should find himself in a more humble and grateful frame of mind.

One morning, all "un-uniformed," Hans rode to town with his master. His task was to search the shops for a certain piece of silk for the nobleman's lady to embroider as a bookmark for her Bible.

While his master refreshed himself at the tavern, Hans happened to fall in with a group of German pilgrims who, on hearing his sad story, advised escape. Hans agreed.

For twelve miles he ran the road while the friendly pilgrims helped him by misdirecting his pursuers. At length he reached the home of a weaver who offered him lodging and a job. Being the son of a weaver, Hans knew enough about this craft to be a good assistant to his benefactor. But he dared not stay; he feared his captors were still after him. So he kept on traveling toward home, stopping only to work in order to pay for his lodgings and then up and off again as soon as possible. On the last lap of his journey he seems to have behaved rather dishonestly, posing as a rich youth who had been robbed, whose family would gladly pay well for his safe return. This ruse got him a ride as far as Nürnberg, the original town to which he had set out with Willi. There he slipped away from the coach and continued his journey on foot.

Reaching home safely, he found that his father had died and his mother had remarried. His new stepfather apprenticed him to a tailor for whom he had to work from four in the morning until midnight! Moreover, the tailor was so mean that Hans was obliged to steal wax from the church candles with which to wax his sewing thread—a double sin, in Hans's eyes.

At last, giving in to his pleading, his stepfather sent him to a nearby school. And now Donatus's grammar, which had been sleeping in the back of his brain, all came back to him—but with a burst of understanding. Swiftly he learned to read and write and in due time became the head of a monastery. He wrote several books that were probably more important—although surely less beguiling—than the account of his adventures as a wandering scholar.

His old schoolmaster, the one who had beaten him so violently as a child, now came humbly to apologize. Abbot Hans graciously forgave him. He himself took to teaching little boys their Latin—more gently, one imagines, because of his own misfortunes in search of an education.

A School of the Renaissance

How great a soul is lodged in this little body!

—Pope Eugenius IV

In the 1300s there began in Italy that glorious period in history known as the Renaissance. The word means rebirth and designates a span of about three hundred years when the arts flourished in Europe as they had not done since the Golden Age of Greece.

No one can explain why this creative impulse burst forth at this time and place. It was certainly not the result of peace and tranquility; Italy at the time was a land of warring city-states and power-hungry nobles. Some scholars claim that Italy, as the center of trade, was stimulated by new ideas from the East; others believe that the rise of wealth among people of taste provided a market for beauty; still others explain that the medieval universities, for all their limitations, had encouraged people to think, and that therefore such an awakening was bound to take place somewhere, and that Italy was closest to the ancient glories of Rome. But whatever the reason, the Renaissance did occur, and we can be grateful for its gifts to civilization.

It was a time, above all, of life and vigor. It was as if man had been living the life of an invalid for many hundreds of years, patiently and fearfully saying his prayers, taking his medicines, and then one day had suddenly awakened feeling well and strong. He looked at the world about him—at trees, at strong-limbed men and beautiful women, at cool fruits, at fine materials, at children playing—and delighted in them all. He looked up to the heavens, and his eyes saw a God and bright angels who wished him to love his gift of life. He felt an urge to express that love. He painted pictures of the beauties around him as he saw them, and of the saints and angels as he imagined them. He honored the human form in sculptures huge in size and breathtaking in their balance. He wrote and sang of joys and sorrows.

Along with this rebirth of the arts rose an interest in the knowledge of the ancients, often referred to as the "revival of learning." Not only scholars but men of wealth contributed to this revival. Indeed, it was their enthusiasm—and of course their money—that made it all possible. Princes and nobles who had cared more for polished armor than for polished minds now became patrons of arts and letters. They collected old manuscripts, unearthing original classics that for centuries had been hidden away in the vaults of monasteries. They employed artists to paint pictures on their palace walls and to decorate churches with masterpieces in paint, marble, bronze, and gold. Many of them housed poets and scholars, musicians and clowns in their palaces. And they vied with each other in procuring fine teachers for their children.

One such noble was Gian Francesco Gonzaga, the marchese of Mantua. Gonzaga had five children, three boys and two girls, for whom he had ambitions. Unfortunately—or perhaps fortunately for posterity—the eldest son, Ludovico, was fat, lazy, and seemingly stupid. His tutors despaired of him; at the age of fifteen all he cared about was eating, sleeping, and lolling about in comfort. On the other hand Carlo, the second son, was thin and nervous. When the marchese heard that a certain schoolmaster in Venice was clever with difficult boys, he urged him to come as tutor to the Mantua palace.

A School of the Renaissance

The schoolmaster's name was Vittorino Ramboldini. But he was always called Vittorino da Feltre—"little Vittorio from Feltre," his native town at the foot of the Alps. He was a short, slender man who dressed in a scholar's dark robe and sandals. He had a gentle voice but firm ideas about teaching.

He hesitated to become a palace tutor. He had no wish to cater to the spoiled children of nobility or to their parents. At his own school in Venice he had been taking promising sons of poor parents as well as lads of wealth. His answer to the marchese was that if he was to teach the Gonzaga children, it must be at a school of his own ordering, outside the palace, and attended by other boys of his own choosing.

The marchese agreed. He offered Vittorino his handsome villa, La Gioia, which had been built outside the city as a vacation palace. *La Gioia* means pleasure house, and the villa was certainly a pleasant spot. Its approach was a tree-lined avenue cutting through wide meadows—fine playing fields, Vittorino decided, for active boys. Its lawn sloped down to a free-flowing river, clean and not too swift—a perfect spot, he thought, for boys to swim. Vittorino returned to Venice, packed up, and came to Mantua.

His first step was to refurnish the villa. It had been sumptuously outfitted, as befitted a palace, with rich hangings, soft divans, and costly objects of art. Its walls were painted with charming frescoes of birds and animals and children at play. These frescoes, with the view of the lawns and river, were enough luxury for a school; the silks and velvets and rich furniture were removed.

His next step was to change the name of the villa to La Giocosa—the happy house. And that name is important in the history of schools. For La Giocosa was the first school, since the days of ancient Greece, where children were meant to be happy.

Not that Vittorino was indulgent. His idea of a happy boy was not a spoiled boy or a loutish boy or even an overstudious bookworm. The wiry little man was a great stickler for good carriage: his boys must stand up straight and proud. A boy who slouched was made to stand stiffly within a chalked circle for an hour while his schoolmates played games. Nor did he allow many creature comforts in the villa. Even though winters can be cold in northern Italy, La Giocosa had no open fires. If a boy's teeth chattered, Vittorino advised him to jump up and down or to sing a psalm at the top of his lungs to warm his vitals. Rich foods were forbidden, as were feather beds and the fur-trimmed garments and furbelows that usually clothed young princelings of the day. Servants who were found slipping such luxuries to the students were dismissed.

On the other hand, Vittorino permitted no beating. Forsaking the old Roman idea that a boy's ears were on his back and only the switch could make him hear, he felt that school should be carried on in a spirit of good will. Ill temper was his bugbear. As Alcuin had confessed to the sin of laziness in his youth, so Vittorino, the soul of gentleness, confessed to an early bad temper. With his strong will for self-control he had conquered his fault; now he would not allow himself or anyone else to raise a hand in anger against one of his pupils.

Boys who could not live up to his standards were simply returned to their parents.

But the boys who stayed had a good time. At monastic schools, we remember, games had been frowned upon as a waste of time, but at La Giocosa those broad fields came alive with sports. Running races, wrestling, archery, and even a primitive kind of football kept the boys active. There was dancing indoors in bad weather; and in summer there were swims in the river and mountain climbing in his beloved Venetian Alps led by Vittorino himself. With all this exercise, even Ludovico, slow-witted and flabby, became a new boy.

The news of Vittorino's school spread. Pupils were sent to him from as far away as Germany. As before, Vittorino accepted a number of boys who could pay no fee; from his own pocket he paid for their board and clothing. The school grew to an enrollment of seventy scholars—an immense number for

a court school. Vittorino had to employ other teachers to help him.

It was an oddly assorted school. The pupils ranged in age from six to twenty-seven (not counting the little Gonzaga girls, who each started at the age of four. Cecilia, indeed, was Vittorino's pride. She started to learn Greek when she was six; by the time she was eight, she could write "elegantly" in both Greek and Latin!).

As in church schools and universities, lessons were carried on in Latin. Latin was the language of scholarship; Latin, it was believed, would always be the language of the courts. It was important for young gentlemen to speak it correctly. But before we shed tears of pity for the Renaissance boys, we must remember that Latin was not so different from their native tongue. The Italian language had developed from the Latin and was about as close to it as today's English is to the language of Chaucer. To the German boys, Latin presented more of a problem—but that was why they went to school.

Much of the learning was still by rote. There were no printed books as yet, and handwritten ones were scarce and very valuable. Vittorino, wanting his students to love learning, tried to make the lessons palatable. The beginners learned their alphabet by means of letter games, their simple arithmetic by means of counting games. Latin prayers and psalms they learned by heart, but with full understanding of their meaning. Recitations could not be babbled off; Vittorino required reverence and good diction.

Tales from Greek and Roman mythology, so long forbidden by the medieval church, were read at La Giocosa for their content of courage and adventure. Vittorino imported native Greeks to teach that language. While he deeply admired the works of Homer and Pindar, Aristotle and Plato and Plutarch, he was not fluent enough in Greek to teach it himself.

Through reading, grammar, and long passages learned by heart for their style, the boys were soon writing their own poetry and prose in Latin and Greek. Gianlucido Gonzaga, the marchese's third son, at the age of fourteen composed two hundred lines of Latin poetry in honor of the emperor's visit to Mantua—a feat that amazed the visiting dignitaries, if not Vittorino.

Geometry was taught by a Greek who was familiar with the works of Euclid. It was a practical sort of geometry, based more on drawing and measuring than on learning theorems by heart. A music teacher instructed pupils in playing the lute and the lyre—although Vittorino, perhaps out of respect for his own ears, allowed only musically talented boys to take the subject. Other studies were history, gleaned from the writings of Plutarch (in Greek) and Livy (in Latin), a little natural history, a little astronomy. The human mind was awakening to the excitement of science, an awareness that the great painter Leonardo da Vinci was soon to express in his art.

All the boys at La Giocosa were not so brilliant as the Gonzaga children. Vittorino did not expect them to be. He felt that it was unfair to require all the youths to have the same interests and encouraged each boy to follow his bent. A writer of the time remembered how "Vittorino, now well advanced in years, would of a winter's morning come early, candle in one hand and a book in the other, and rouse a pupil in whose progress he was specially interested; he would leave him time to dress, waitingly patiently till he was ready: then he would hand him the book, and encourage him with grave and earnest words to higher endeavor."

But he would not allow overwork. When, during playtime, he came upon two boys earnestly discussing the past lesson, he chided, "This is not a good sign in a young boy," and sent them off to join in the game.

Vittorino's school, small as it was, made a mark in history. Among its graduates were princes and nobles who were famous for their wise leadership. Others were simply proud examples of "the Renaissance man"—men of learning, courage, and, above all, honor.

But apart from its immediate effect on the princes of Italy

and their subjects, La Giocosa brought fresh air into the stuffy cells of learning. Boys and girls of today, who take for granted the encouragement of their teachers and their own right to health and play, can be grateful to Vittorino for his firm idea of what a school should be.

The Dame School

And there sat by the empty fireplace, which was filled with a pot of sweet herbs, the nicest old woman that ever was seen, in her red petticoat, and short dimity bedgown, and clean white cap, with a black silk handkerchief over it, tied under her chin. At her feet sat the grandfather of all the cats, and opposite her sat, on two benches, twelve or fourteen neat, rosy, chubby little children, learning their Chris-cross row; and gabble enough they made about it. . . .

—*The Water Babies*, CHARLES KINGSLEY

Those who have read *The Water Babies* will remember this as the scene that met the feverish eyes of Tom the chimney sweep when, fleeing across the northern English moors, he scrabbled down Lewthwaite Crag to seek refuge in the little cottage a thousand feet below. The classroom into which he stumbled was a dame school, a kind of elementary school that had sprung up in England in the sixteenth century. And the "Chris-cross row" that the children were gabbling was the first row of a *printed* alphabet.

It was the invention of printing that gave rise to these cozy little schools. "Everybody now wants to read and write!" marveled an early printer—as though literacy were a new fad, like cycling or tea drinking. And all because a clever inventor named Johann Gutenberg, of the city of Mainz in Germany, had invented the printing press. Considering how greatly this invention affected the lives of all mankind, it is worth glancing at its story.

Gutenberg was not the first to try his hand at printing. For hundreds of years the Chinese had been carving their writing symbols on wood to print on pages. But their woodblock method was no closer to what we call letterpress printing than is a rubber stamp to a printing press. It took a Gutenberg to invent movable type, a method of fastening it in place, and a way of transferring the inked letters onto pages of paper.

The process of papermaking was already known in Europe. It had been brought to Spain by those useful Arabs who, during their invasions, spread so much Oriental knowledge. In 1340 a paper mill had been started in Spain; others soon followed in Italian cities; and by 1450 the delicious novelty, blank sheets of paper ready to be inked with words, was available throughout Europe.

As do most inventors, Gutenberg had his troubles. In 1456, in great secrecy and with the help of his personally trained assistants, he printed his first book. The book was the Bible. Its making was a long process, involving six presses working at the same time. The pages were "illuminated," their margins decorated with colored pictures and designs to look as much as possible like the manuscript works hand-copied and hand-painted by monks. Such close copying hoped to keep secret the fact of printing.

However, since some three hundred copies of the Gutenberg Bible were printed, the secret could not be kept for long. Mainz became known as the home of the miraculous new art. And a neighboring duke, Adolf of Nassau, brought an army to seize the city, as dukes did in those days, in order to grab the printing industry for himself. But Gutenberg's printers managed to flee the city in time, carrying with them the secrets of their craft.

Soon they set up printing presses in other parts of the Continent. So Adolf's greed merely spread printing sooner throughout Europe.

And now printed pamphlets gushed from the presses, papering the cities with words. To be able to read was no longer a scholar's accomplishment; it was a necessity. In the new world of the published word, to be unable to read was like being deaf at a concert. Reformers urged that all children be taught to read—not only the sons of nobles or boys destined for a profession—and that they be taught to read not in scholarly Latin, but in their own tongue.

The reformers were not heeded at once. Indeed, during the Reformation of the sixteenth century, schooling in England was at a low ebb. Monasteries were shut down, and the Roman Catholic priests, who had taught children in connection with the church or cathedral, were scattered. But the eagerness to read and write had been planted. The printing of schoolbooks had started. And in the towns and villages, the small children of even quite humble families were led to the cottage of the local "dame" to learn their lessons.

The dame had no special training as a teacher. The poet George Crabbe has described her as a "deaf poor patient widow"; but of course she was not necessarily either deaf or widowed. Patient she must have been, to cope with a number of small children; and if she happened to be deaf, it only made her task less nerve-wracking. Poor she undoubtedly was; she was paid very little, and sometimes only in gifts of food or goods. But she was educated well enough to know her letters and her catechism; and these she managed to drill into the heads of her small pupils.

Their first "book" was a hornbook made of a flat piece of wood shaped like a butter paddle. To this was fastened a paper printed with reading matter, and over it a thin sheet of horn, almost as thin and transparent as modern plastic, to preserve it from grubby hands. Many thrifty parents bored a hole through the handle of their child's hornbook and strung it with a leather thong about their young scholar's neck to prevent him from losing it.

The first lesson of the hornbook was the alphabet. At the beginning of the first line was printed a +, symbol of the cross of Christ; thus the first line became known as the Chris-cross row. At the start of his lesson the child made the sign of the cross on his small chest, murmured: "In the name of the Father, and of the Son, and of the Holy Ghost," and went on to do battle with the letters of the alphabet. After the letters came simple syllables, and finally the Lord's Prayer: "Our Father which art in Heaven . . ."

When a child had mastered his hornbook—no doubt by heart—he graduated to the primer. This was an actual book, bound in stout wooden covers and filled with solemn religious matters. But as printing was perfected, pictures were added to the text. Printers found that by cutting woodblocks of the same depth as their type and by locking them into the framed plate of words, they could print simple pictures along with the text. The pictures were not colored and gay, as in primers of today. But they were pictures, and often exciting ones, and must have encouraged many small brains to get on with the lesson. And the text, stuffy and moral as it was and in print that was difficult to read, was at least in English instead of Latin—not English as we know it, for any language changes with the years; but it was English as the children were used to hearing it spoken.

Many dames could also teach counting. This was naturally done by using the fingers. Sometimes lines were drawn in sand, and pebbles used as counters. Older children might learn addition on a ruled board—the "counter" that was used in a shop. For what we now call a store counter, on which goods are displayed and sales slips written up, was originally such a board marked with lines to represent pounds, shillings, and pence. Wooden checkers, called "counting pennies," were moved from square to square to arrive at totals.

Not the least of the dame's tasks was to teach behavior. Her

pupils must learn obedience and good manners. The little boys must bow and the little girls curtsy; both must speak up when spoken to. Indeed, the good dame had to be a combination of teacher, governess, and baby sitter, for many of her pupils were brought to her as soon as they could toddle, merely to keep them out of mischief while their mothers worked. But it seems that she was able to handle it all quite capably, knitting busily all the while. As Crabbe explained:

> Her room is small, they cannot widely stray,—
> Her threshold high, they cannot run away;
> Though deaf, she sees the rebel-heroes shout,—
> Though lame, her white rod nimbly walks about:
>
> With band of yarn she keeps offenders in,
> And to her gown the sturdiest rogue can pin;
> Aided by these, and spells, and tell-tale birds,
> Her powers they dread, and reverence her words.

Other poets besides Crabbe wrote affectionately of the dame schoolteacher. With her knitting yarn, her "little birds" who told tales on little people, and no doubt eyes in the back of her head, she became an institution in English villages and was a godsend to busy mothers for many centuries.

Not all small English boys and girls attended a dame school. The children of wealthy parents were taught their letters at home, while children whose parents worked in the fields had to forgo booklearning for the lore of livestock and crops. But the little school gave increasing numbers of ordinary children a chance to learn to read their own language for a small fee. And informal as it was, the dame school was the ancestor of the English and American primary school.

A Sixteenth-Century
English Boys' School

Wherefore I praye you, all lytel babys, all lytel chyl-
dren, lerne gladly this lytel treatyse, and commende
it dyly gently unto your memoryes. . . . And lyfte up
your lytel whyte handes for me, which prayeth for
you to God.
                              —from a preface by JOHN COLET

The "lytel treatyse" prefaced by these lines was nothing more
exciting than a book of Latin grammar. And the "lytel babys"
and "lytel chyldren" to whom it was so lovingly addressed
were schoolboys of sixteenth-century England. Since these
boys were of high-school age, their hands were probably not so
very little nor often very white. But John Colet, the dean of
Saint Paul's Cathedral in London, was an idealist. He not only
founded a new and different kind of school for boys; he paid
for it out of his own pocket until he ran out of funds. He died
impoverished but probably gratified by his accomplishment.

Grammar schools for boys had long existed in connection
with cathedrals and monasteries. Some of them in existence

today can trace their beginnings to the times when England was under Roman rule. As we have seen in the account of monastic schools, their discipline had been heavy and their teachings limited.

But John Colet had been to Italy. There his mind was fired by the revival of classical learning and by the philosophy called "humanism" because of its interest in humanity as well as heaven. He got permission from King Henry VIII to revive the old cathedral school—the School of Saint Paul's Churchyard, it had been called—along new lines. Here young Londoners were to be given their chance at the "new learning"— that is, the ancient classics.

With his own rules as well as his own funds, Dean Colet set up his school. He appointed the Mercers' Company, a guild of businessmen, as trustees. It was now a "public school," which in England means not a free school but a school not under the control of the church. But Saint Paul's, endowed by Colet himself, was actually free—except for an enrollment fee of four pence, to be given to the "poor scholar" whose job it was to sweep the floors. The number of scholars was limited to 153 in order to coincide with the number of fishes netted from the sea in the Biblical miracle (John 21:11). And to this day, scholarship boys at Saint Paul's wear a small silver fish on their watch chains.

To be admitted, boys had to be able to read and write at least well enough to manage their lessons. Their parents were required to provide them with books, writing materials, and good wax candles (not tallow candles, stipulated the dean, which were both drippy and smelly) to light their work during the long, dark days of winter. School was to be held from seven to eleven in the morning and from one to five in the afternoon, winter and summer. There were to be no sudden holidays ("remedyes," they were called), which, it seems, weary or sporting priests had been fond of announcing; and any master found awarding such holidays was to be fined—"excepte the Kyng, or an Archbishop, or a Bishop present in his own person at the Scole desire it"—an exception which must have made such visitors very popular with the boys. Nor might boys be absent for any reason except sickness; and if they were sick often or for long, they must forfeit their places in the school to healthier lads. Moreover, if, after a fair trial, a boy proved too slow at his lessons, his parents were asked to remove him from the school so as to waste neither his time nor the teachers'.

Dean Colet then collected his masters, awarding them an unusually high salary both in money and in bolts of cloth for their clothing. He persuaded his friend Desiderius Erasmus, the great humanist scholar, to write some textbooks, and appointed as his headmaster William Lily, author of *Lily's Latin Grammar*, to which the dean himself wrote the prayerful introduction. Dry and pinched as that little book appears today, at the time it was considered a marvel of clear text. Henry VIII was so impressed that he ordered it to be the official textbook in all schools throughout his realm! It remained the principal schoolbook of thousands of boys for hundreds of years.

For Dean Colet, like other humanists, was an enthusiast for correct Latin. He was disgusted by the garbled, sloppy state into which the language had fallen in the church schools: he called it "blotterature" rather than literature. Good Latin and Greek were to be the first principles of Saint Paul's boys.

"I wolde that they were taught all way in good litterature both laten and greke," he directed in the language and spelling of the times, "and good auctours [authors] suych as have the very Romayne eliquence joyned with wisdome, specially Christyn auctours that wrote theyre wisdome with clene and chast laten other in verse or in prose, for my entent is by this scole specially to increase knowledge and worshipping of God and our lorde Crist Jesu and goode cristen lyffe and maners in the Children."

The school building was across the street from Saint Paul's Cathedral. There, shortly before seven in the morning, the boys gathered and filed their way into the schoolrooms. They took their places on the tiers of wooden benches, or forms, which lined the walls. They sat according to their grades, the younger ones at the front and the older ones on the higher forms in the rear. From this seating came the term *form*, meaning class or grade, which is still used in many English schools and in some American ones (a beginner being a "first former," and so on). In each form one boy was appointed as its president—perhaps a first step toward student government.

The high master (or principal) and the surmaster (his assistant) were both laymen and both married—a distinct departure from the schools in which all teaching had been done by priests. Two "ushers" taught the lower forms.

This is not to say that the school was not deeply religious. The morning session opened with prayers; the afternoon session opened with prayers; and at five o'clock the boys knelt in prayer before going home. Moreover, a priest was employed to sing a daily Mass in the chapel of the school and to "pray for the Children to prosper in good lyff and in goode litterature. At his masse when the bell in the Scole shall knyll [ring] to sacryng [worship]," ordered the dean, "thenne all the children in the scole knelynge in theyr settes shal with lift upp handes pray in the time of sacryng. After the sacryng whenne the bell knylleth again, they shall sitt downe ageyn to theyr bokes lernyng."

And what was the subject taught in this new kind of school? Latin, Latin, and more Latin. Verb endings, tenses, phrases, sentences, conversation, prose, and poetry. The younger boys plugged away at Lily's *Grammar*, and at memorizing words and simple sentences—*vulgaria*, they were called. A small boy had to be smart at this memorizing, for he knew that in a short time he would have to talk entirely in Latin, even at play. A boy above the first form who was overheard speaking English was given a black mark, and a number of black marks meant a flogging!

But as the boys progressed in Latin, they were given the books that marked Saint Paul's as new and daring. For besides some early Christian "auctours" who wrote in Latin, they now read the poets Horace, Ovid, and Vergil, the historian Sallust, the orator Cicero, and the playwright Terence.

Older churchmen threw up their hands in horror. School-boys allowed to read the pagan Vergil's epic about the Trojan hero Aeneas! The odes of Horace, praising nature and human pleasures! The poems of Ovid, recounting pre-Christian tales and legends! The plays of Terence, filled with rogues and plot and fun! Such a school, thundered the Bishop of London, was nothing less than "a temple of idolatry." Twice he tried to convict the gentle Dean Colet of heresy and to shut down the school. But no one could really prove that a school that taught so much of the Christian religion was actually anti-Christian. Besides, the classics were by now the major subjects of study in the universities. The "revival of learning" was here to stay.

Upper-form boys were set to Greek. Indeed, Erasmus had advised that Greek and Latin be learned simultaneously from the beginning; but headmaster Lily apparently thought this would be too confusing. His boys had to be fluent in Latin before starting Greek; in fact the rules of their Greek grammar were written in Latin. For those who were struggling with Greek a favorite exercise was to translate Aesop's fables from Greek into English, from English into Latin, and from Latin back into Greek—a task that no doubt kept them from entirely forgetting the English language.

By now the boys were so fluent in Latin that they could not only write Latin compositions and poetry, but make jokes and carry on debates in the tongue. A high spot in the school was a sort of classical contest held on the Eve of Saint Bartholomew (August 23). On that summer night the boys from different London schools gathered in Saint Bartholomew's Churchyard to "dispute" or debate in both Latin and Greek.

The competition was a rather uproarious affair. The boys not only made rough jokes about each other, but composed clever rhymes making fun of their masters—using no names, of course; and inevitably the contest turned into a roughhouse. Although the dean disapproved of this annual event, calling it a "foolish babbling and a losse of time," it went on just the same; and Saint Paul's boys proved to be the cleverest of the lot.

Another pleasant break in the humdrum of grammar and syntax was acting plays in Latin. The boys put on the robust comedies of Terence for the public, and even for royalty, to much applause. Later in the century they were even allowed to put on plays in English, plays written expressly to be performed by "the Children of St. Paule's School." So excellent were these performances that the playwright Ben Jonson complained that the schoolmasters were making "all their schollers Playboyes!"

Athletic games, too, began to play a real part in school life. This was another departure from monastic school ways—and, indeed, from English custom. As recently as 1365 King Edward III had banned "unthrifty and idle games" throughout the kingdom under pain of punishment. But times were changing. In Italy humanism had followed Vittorino's approval of games; and Dean Colet had been to Italy. At Saint Paul's and the other grammar schools that followed its lead, boys were encouraged in the classical exercises of running and wrestling, as well as in leapfrog and a favorite English sport, archery. Fives, a game of handball played against a wall, was a popular sport. Another game, called stoolball, played with a stick, is said to be the ancestor of cricket, the national sport of England. Even a crude kind of football was encouraged at Saint Paul's, although some other schools outlawed it as too rough.

During all such games the boys had to speak in Latin. More important, they had to "play the game" with self-control and good manners. For in these public schools was born the fine English tradition of good sportsmanship: to play fair, to do one's best, and to be a gracious loser.

Good manners were insisted on throughout the school day. The sixteenth century in England was a violent one, filled with wars and power struggles and beheadings. But in the grammar schools, at least, politeness prevailed. These boys, from whatever walk of life they had come, were being trained to be gentlemen. They had to stand up and bow to their elders. They had

to walk quietly in the streets, and not "practise any games which are not of a gentlemanly appearance and free of all lowness." One boarding school expressly stated its rules for table manners: students must cut their bread with their knives, not gnaw at it with their teeth or tear at it with their nails; nor should they drink with their mouths full, nor pick their teeth with their knives! Saint Paul's, a day school that allowed no eating or drinking on its grounds, had no such problems with table manners. But black marks were given for shouting in the building, for untidiness, and for soiled clothing.

Discipline was strict and beatings were many. Vittorino's ideas were not followed in this respect; western Europe still believed that the switch was the best aid to memory. Floggings were administered for bad lessons as well as for bad behavior.

A graduate of Saint Paul's wrote: "The misery I had at Grammar School was very great by reason of my unaptness [slowness at books]. The said Cook [headmaster at the time] with lashes set more than seven scars on my hide which still remain." Another principal of Saint Paul's had such a temper that he seized a slow pupil by the ears and dragged him round and round the schoolroom until a softhearted usher interfered.

Other schools were just as severe, if not worse. At Eton during the reign of Queen Elizabeth the boys took to running away in droves; the queen's secretary confided to her that this exodus might just possibly be the result of too much flogging. But most English schoolboys of the time, and for generations to come, accepted the floggings along with the Latin and prayers and games as the normal lot of boyhood.

Latin and Greek were the only subjects taught at Saint Paul's and other grammar schools in those early days. No science; no mathematics; no geography; and no history (except for such outdated bits as cropped up in the classics).

This lack seems particularly sad when we consider what exciting advances in knowledge were under way. Columbus had recently discovered an unknown hemisphere. Magellan's ship had sailed around the globe. The astronomer Copernicus was busily charting the motions of the earth and the planets. The Italian artist Leonardo da Vinci had been stirred to fascinating discoveries in human anatomy and vision, in the laws of hydraulics, and in the dynamics of engineering. At the universities, men's minds had been triggered to question, to experiment, to discover. But the noses of schoolboys were kept to the grindstone of ancient classics.

At the beginning, this insistence on Latin and Greek was not as useless as it may seem. The languages were beautiful; they were also useful. Latin was still the international language of knowledge. The explorers mapped out their plans from voyagers' accounts written in Latin. Latin was the written language of the law, of medicine, of the town hall, of the merchant. And ancient Greek writings were still the springboards to the sciences. Thus, in the early days of the sixteenth century, it was necessary to know Latin and Greek before going on to other subjects.

But many grammar schools kept up their limited curriculum long after its practical usefulness was over. As late as 1824—more than three hundred years after Dean Colet had outlined his school courses—a headmaster told a parent firmly: "At St. Paul's we teach nothing but the classics, nothing but Latin and Greek. If you want your son to learn anything else you must have him taught at home, and for this purpose we give him three half-holidays a week."

Girls in sixteenth-century England did not go to school. Wealthy families might employ tutors for their daughters to teach them music and singing and book learning. Queen Elizabeth, as a child, was called a brilliant scholar by her tutors; and she certainly encouraged the arts and explorations during her reign. But few girls had her advantages. Most of them learned only from their mothers, who taught them to cook, to sew, to be devout Christians, and to make themselves generally useful and charming.

At least they escaped all those floggings.

Extras: Writing and Ciphering

Scholars almost ready to go to the University have been found who could hardly tell the numbers of the pages, sections, chapters and other divisions in their books.

—JOHN BRINSLEY, schoolmaster c. 1600

For many hundreds of years, as we have seen, the church had frowned on science. The natural laws of the universe had been held to be the business of God, not of human beings. To the Christians, the pagan Arab symbols used in mathematics and geometry smacked of alchemy and astrology and witchcraft. Even Martin Luther, the famous reformer who founded the Lutheran Church, preached against the discoveries of Copernicus.

"A devil in the telescope," he cried, "deceives the eye!"

A mathematician named John Dee was accused of dabbling in the black arts because he wrote a book about geometry. "O Brainsicke, Rashe, Spiteful and Disdainfull Countrymen!" he pleaded. "Why oppresse you me, thus violently, with your slandering of me?"

Extras: Writing and Ciphering

Even simple arithmetic was neglected by the grammar schools. The neglect proved uncomfortable. Sixth formers, chattering away in Latin and Greek, could not even read figures or do simple sums. Something had to be done.

Some grammar schools started offering arithmetic as an extra. It was taught by a special teacher (the classics masters being quite ignorant of the subject themselves) who came to the school for an afternoon or two a week. Other schools, like Saint Paul's, simply gave their students two or three half-holidays a week in which to go to the teacher of these mysteries.

There was a choice of two kinds of arithmetic: casting accounts and ciphering. Casting accounts was done with counters as in the dame school. This was practiced by boys who expected to go into trade. Ciphering was working out sums on paper; it was advised for boys who planned to go on to a university.

Ciphering was not easy for a grammar-school boy. In the first place, the Arabic numerals 1, 2, 3, 4, 5, 6, 7, 8, 9, 0, which today we learn with the alphabet, had only recently reached England. The old Roman numerals were still used for the pages of books; the new ones were unfamiliar.

Also, there were no multiplication tables. It seems almost unbelievable that in an age when so much was learned by rote, children of high-school age had not learned to chant their "twice times" and their "seven times." But such tables, it seems, had never been worked out. Sums in multiplication, whether worked by counters or on paper, were simply done by addition.

A Mr. Robert Recorde wrote a book of arithmetic that was for long the standard—if not the only—textbook. He is said to have been the first to use the symbols +, —, ×, and =; before him, there had only been the words *plus, minus,* and so on. He also presented a very ingenious way of multiplying. To multiply 7 × 8, you wrote the 8 under the 7 thus: 7. Next you
8

subtracted each of these numbers from 10 and set the difference beside it: 7 3. The next step was to multiply (by addition) the
8 2

figures in the right-hand column; 3 × 2 gave you 6, which you wrote below it: 7 3. The last step was to subtract cross-

$$\begin{array}{cc} 8 & 2 \\ \hline & 6 \end{array}$$

wise the 3 from the 8 or the 2 from the 7, either of which gave you the number 5. This you wrote beneath the left-hand figures: 7 3. And lo and behold, you had found that 7 × 8 is

$$\begin{array}{cc} 8 & 2 \\ \hline 5 & 6 \end{array}$$

56! If the units figure in the right-hand column was higher than 10, you simply carried it over to the tens column: 7 3

$$\begin{array}{cc} 6 & 4 \\ \hline 4 & 2 \end{array}$$

If the numbers to be multiplied were greater than 10, you would put down the difference between each number and 10— 12 2—and then add crosswise, instead of subtracting, to get

13 3

the answer: 12 2

$$\begin{array}{cc} 13 & 3 \\ \hline 15 & 6 \end{array}$$

A most roundabout way to multiply; but it works!

But such "ciphering," or "pen arithmetic" as it was often called, was only tackled by boys heading for a university. At least it taught them how to write down numerals.

Penmanship was the other extra with which boys were tortured on Wednesday or Saturday afternoons. Again, it seems surprising that the art of writing by hand was left alone for so long. But, heretofore, writing had mostly been done by monks or by paid professional scriveners. The handwriting of even an educated man was pretty illegible. Now, with paper in general use and written assignments the daily rule at grammar schools, teachers understandably began to be concerned about the boys' handwriting. It was they, after all, who had to read and correct the written exercises. It was decided that the young scholars' Latin must be not only correct but legible.

Extras: Writing and Ciphering

But nothing, it seems, was made easy for the sixteenth-century schoolboy. His writing lessons were in three different scripts: the English script, called *secretary*; the Roman; and the Greek. (Later on in the century, studies in Hebrew were offered at Saint Paul's, and students had to learn that script also.) He had copybooks in each of these kinds of writing and spent his half-holidays at the inky task of practicing them all.

His writing tool was a quill pen made from a goosefeather. Even the best of these soon split, sputtered, and gave out. Mending pens by cutting a new point on them with a penknife or making out-and-out new ones was a duty of the writing master. John Brinsley, the schoolmaster who had deplored the boys' ignorance of numbers, urged that everyone know how to make his own pen in case he wished to use it when no writing master was at hand. Mr. Brinsley wrote explicit directions for pen-making:

1. Choose the quil of the best and strongest of the wing, which is somewhat harder and will cleave [split].
2. Make it cleane, with the back of your pen-knife.
3. Cleave it straight up the back, first with a cleft made with your pen-knife: after, with another quil put into it, rive [split] it further, little by little and little, till you see the cleft to be veray cleane: so you may make your pen of the best of the quil, where you see the cleft to be cleanest, with no teeth. . .

and so on.

Paper was still scarce and expensive. Nobody wasted paper. Sheets that had been written on were saved and used for wrapping, and often, afterward, as cleaning rags. Permanent notebooks were still made of parchment, more durable than paper. In these the boys wrote, in their best writing, the Latin and Greek words, phrases, and sentences that they would use again and again in writing and speaking.

Schools of Hard Knocks: Apprenticeships and Charity Schools

Nobody did he see but a big charity-boy, sitting on a post in front of the house, eating a slice of bread and butter.... "Yer don't know who I am, I suppose, Work'us?" said the charity-boy...." "No, sir," rejoined Oliver.

—*Oliver Twist*, CHARLES DICKENS

Oliver Twist, you will remember, was an orphan who had spent the first ten years of his life in a workhouse, a shelter where the very poor were housed and put to work. There he had disgraced himself by asking for more gruel. The authorities, appalled at this impudence, had apprenticed him to Mr. Sowerby, an undertaker. Mr. Sowerby was to be paid five pounds " 'upon liking,'—a phrase," explains Dickens, "which means, in the case of a parish apprentice, that if the master find, upon a short trial, that he can get enough work out of a boy without putting too much food into him, he shall have him for a term of years, to do what he likes with."

The apprenticeship system had been going on in England since the thirteenth century. Like chivalry, it was not an actual school; but like chivalry, it was a customary way to train boys for their future careers. A lad worked for free for a master while learning that master's trade. Ordinarily the choice of the master was up to the boy's family; they might choose a weaver, or a shoemaker, or a carpenter, or a blacksmith, or any other artisan to teach their son. Such craftsmen had their workshops in their own homes; like the nobles with their would-be knights, they took the boys to live with them as part of the family, and fed and clothed and taught them their prayers as well as their craft.

Generally, apprentices were well treated. There are as many stories of cruel masters as there are of brutal schoolmasters and wicked stepmothers; such evil characters, of course, make a tale more exciting. But there is no reason to believe that master craftsmen, as a group, were ogres, or that their apprentices were long-suffering victims.

At the beginning, the apprenticeship contract was merely a personal agreement between the boy's family and his chosen master. But as towns and businesses increased, the craftsmen formed guilds whose members agreed upon certain rules concerning their craft. To keep up standards of workmanship, a law was enacted in 1563 that prevented a person from becoming a master of a trade until he had been apprenticed to it for seven years. Now each master and each apprentice had to sign papers of *indenture*, an agreement between the two. The paper was often torn in two; only if the two pieces fitted exactly together was it proved genuine.

Different guilds had different requirements for apprenticeship. The number of lads who could enter a trade became limited; each master, therefore, could only take on the number of apprentices allowed by his guild.

Apprentice work hours were from six in the morning to six

in the evening, except for Sundays, which were free, and numerous festival days when work stopped at three. Apprentices were not supposed to frequent taverns or gamble or be in the streets after ten o'clock at night. They had to promise to serve their master faithfully, putting his interests above their own.

Masters, on the other hand, had to take good care of their lads. They had to feed and clothe them properly (a certain ironmonger was fined five shillings for allowing his apprentice's hair to grow too long!). They had to discipline their boys to virtue—but not too roughly, or they could be hauled into court and fined and their contracts taken away.

At the end of his seven years' apprenticeship a lad was given, according to agreement, a new suit of clothes, a pair or two of shoes, a little pocket money, even perhaps some tools for use in his trade. He was now a licensed journeyman and could work for wages for other masters. But this did not mean that he was a master craftsman himself. The guilds limited their membership; no one wanted to send prices down by allowing too many people to ply any one trade. Often a journeyman, for all his skill, remained a hired hand for the rest of his days.

But meanwhile, in merry England, there were many who were worse off than he. In that century of lively happenings— explorers setting forth to chart new lands, new doors opening to commerce, university scholars digging out answers to the mysteries of science, Shakespeare writing his immortal plays, and the sons of gentlemen chattering away in correct Latin— England was becoming very wealthy at the top and very, very poor at the bottom. Beggars, with neither education nor a trade nor a plot of ground to sustain them, were wandering through country lanes and city streets.

"Hark, hark! the dogs do bark! The Beggars are coming to town" was a rhyme written about these vagrants. Countryfolk and townsmen alike feared the rough and desperate beggars. And in 1601 was enacted the famous Poor Law, which required that the poor be rounded up and cared for out of taxes. Workhouses were the grim shelters where folks with no means of support were housed, fed mostly on broth, bread, and gruel, and set to work on "flax, hemp, thread, iron, and other ware and stuff" to earn their meager keep. It was in such a workhouse that Oliver Twist was born and was set to work, at the age of nine, picking oakum—a loose fiber made by untwisting old hemp ropes.

The Poor Law, however, also required that the children of the poor be "bound out," apprenticed, as soon as possible to whatever master would take them.

"Dear me!" said the undertaker's wife, "he's very Small."

"Why, he *is* rather small," replied Mr. Bumble: looking at Oliver as if it were his fault that he was no bigger; "he *is* small. But he'll grow, Mrs. Sowerby—he'll grow."

"Ah! I dare say he will," replied the lady pettishly, "on our victuals and our drink. I see no saving in parish children, not I; for they always cost more to keep, than they're worth. . . ."

Poor children, in fact, were a glut on the market. They had been taught nothing, and they were not very strong. One well-meaning reformer, John Locke, tried to start workhouse schools where children between the ages of three and fourteen might be put to work. This, he thought, would not only make them of some use in the world, but would accustom them at an early age to earn their living. They should be fed, too, on plenty of bread and water—their daily diet at home, only more of it. And on very cold days, he pleaded, they might be given "a little warm water-gruel, if it be thought needful," which wouldn't waste any fuel since it could be cooked on the same stove that heated the building.

The sad little proposal was never carried out. But certain religious groups took the plight of the children to heart and did start up charity schools in the principal cities of England. These were day schools where boys—and even girls—of poor parents were welcomed to learn religion, manners, and certain useful book learning.

Apprenticeships and Charity Schools

Charity schools, like grammar schools, were held from seven to five in the summertime and from eight to four in winter, with two hours off at midday for dinner and chores. As in the grammar schools, too, the day started and ended with prayers. But there the likeness ended. While grammar schools piled on the classics in Latin and Greek, charity schools piled on religion —in English. Two sessions each week were spent on drill in the catechism, a set of formal questions and answers on the beliefs of the Church of England. The schoolmaster was ordered to take great pains to see that the pupils not only pronounced each word distinctly but understood its meaning.

The textbooks for learning to read were the Bible, the prayer book, and works called *The Christian Scholar, The Whole Duty of Man*, and so on. Then came such lessons as were considered useful for boys and girls who were expected to earn their livelihoods.

"As soon as the Boys can read competently well," the program stated, "the Master shall teach them to write a fair legible Hand, with the Grounds of Arithmetick, to fit them for Services or Apprentices."

Girls, however, were not expected to master writing and figuring. Along with reading and religion, they were taught "to knit their Stockings and Gloves, to Mark, Sew, make and mend their Cloaths," sometimes to spin, sometimes even to write a bit. For these were the arts that would help them to be useful as little maids in such households as were willing to take them in.

Meanwhile, particularly strict attention was paid to the manners and morals of charity children. The schoolmaster was directed to "discourage and correct the beginnings of Vice, and particularly Lying, Swearing, Cursing," and playing games on Sunday. The names of the guilty were written down and presented at meetings of the school trustees, who decided on each culprit's punishment or, if he was a repeated sinner, his expulsion from the school.

The schools even provided the children's clothes. These

were special uniforms, carefully chosen for their frugal cost: nine shillings twopence a year for boys, ten shillings threepence for girls. Each year a boy was provided with a new coat, a cap, three "bands" or collars, one pair of stockings, and one pair of shoes. Girls' shoes must have been more perishable; they were allotted two new pairs a year, along with a pair of stockings, two collars, two coifs (a sort of mobcap covering their hair), a gown and petticoat, and a pair of knit gloves. The costumes were neat and rather charming. But they had their drawbacks. For they marked their wearers as "charity children."

"The Children shall wear their Caps, Bands, Cloaths, and other marks of Distinction every day" was the rule, "whereby their Trustees and Benefactors may know them, and see what their behaviour is Abroad."

But other people also recognized the clothes; and more fortunate children were often cruel.

"Noah was a charity-boy, but not a workhouse orphan," explained Dickens in his novel. "The shop-boys in the neighborhood had long been in the habit of branding Noah, in the public streets, with the ignominious epithets of 'Leathers,' 'Charity,' and the like; and Noah had borne them without reply. But, now that fortune had cast in his way a nameless orphan, at whom even the meanest could point the finger of scorn, he retorted on him with interest."

So Noah, the charity-boy apprentice, took out his bitterness on Oliver, the workhouse apprentice, until Oliver's temper broke and he knocked the bully down.

By the time Dickens wrote *Oliver Twist*, workhouses and charity schools had been going on for more than a hundred and fifty years. But they had not changed much in that time; nor would they change for many years to come.

EARLY
MODERN

"Papa" Pestalozzi's Schools

Let the child be a human being, and let the teacher be his friend.

—JOHANN HEINRICH PESTALOZZI

In 1745 in Zurich, Switzerland, a boy was born whose ideas were to change the schools of the world. His name was Johann Heinrich Pestalutz—although he preferred the Italian form of his surname, Pestalozzi.

He was an odd little boy. His father had died when he was five years old, and he was brought up by his devoted mother and her worrisome housekeeper. There was little money to spend on toys and new clothes; Barbeli, the housekeeper, kept the children indoors as much as possible so as to save wear on their coats and shoes. Heinrich did not go to school until he was nine. By then he was an awkward, untidy boy who yearned to make friends.

He was not a quick scholar. His head was full of questions, but in those days schoolchildren were not encouraged to ask questions; he longed to be good at games but was wretched at them; to be a leader, but he only tagged along; to be manly, but he was the class joke. Nor could his mother or Barbeli help him in these ambitions; they could not even keep him neat. He was one of those boys whose garter always broke, whose coat was buttoned wrong, whose mittens did not match. His school-mates called him "Harry Oddity from Foolsville."

But their teasing was affectionate, for he was a good-natured, likable boy. And once, at least, he was a hero. An earthquake tremor had shaken the hillside, rattling the schoolhouse and sending the pupils and masters running for safety. It was little "Harry Oddity" who ventured back into the tottering building to rescue the books and jackets left behind. In his later life, Pestalozzi looked back at this act of daring as the high point of his school career.

The summer months he spent with his grandfather, a pastor in a neighboring town. Together they visited the poor—who, at that time and place, were very poor indeed. The boy was so distressed by the sights of hunger and disease and misery that he grew up determined to help those less fortunate than himself.

His first effort, upon graduating from college, was to become a preacher. But during his trial sermon he became so nervous and stumbled and mumbled so badly that he gave up that career. Next he studied law, thinking that as a lawyer he could champion the rights of the poor. But he was slow at his book and found the studies dull and unrewarding. He decided, instead, to apprentice himself to a farmer who could teach him the principles of agriculture.

In plowing and fertilizing and reaping crops Pestalozzi found contentment. He married a fine young woman, took the little money left to him by his father, borrowed some more, and bought himself a farm. He called it Neuhof (New Farm) and set out to raise madder, a plant whose roots were used in making dye.

NEUHOF

The farm was not successful. Pestalozzi was not a good businessman (it was said that dealers tricked him), and he was soon in debt. He decided to turn his farm into a sort of training school for neglected children.

In those days the children of laborers were often set to work when they were eight years old. With no chance of schooling, they lived like small toiling animals, turning over their earnings to their families or their bosses. Pestalozzi was convinced that with a better start in life these youngsters could grow up to be intelligent citizens. He would teach them to farm efficiently, to read and write, to weave and spin, to use their brains as well as their arms and legs.

He started with some twenty children. They ranged in age from six to eighteen—ragged paupers all. Some were already tough and sly, some thin and sickly, some rosy and dirty. He and his wife took them into their home and treated them like their own children. They washed them up, clothed and fed them, nursed them back to health, and tried, above all, to make them happy. For Pestalozzi believed that children are born good. Love and understanding, he felt, were better teachers' aids than scoldings and switches.

People shook their heads over this strange school. Children, everyone knew, were wicked little creatures who must be beaten into a state of virtue before there was any hope for their souls. They predicted another failure for Pestalozzi.

But the children adored him. They called him "Papa" like his own small son; and to many of them he was the only father they had ever known. They ran to greet him when he came in the door, the older ones seizing his arms, the younger ones hugging his legs. His heart was large enough for all of them.

In summertime he worked with the boys on the farm. He taught them what he had learned of farming: how to fertilize the soil, tend the livestock, care for fruit trees, and work with nature to produce crops. His wife taught the girls home-making: cooking and sewing and keeping the house tidy—the latter a lesson which Papa Pestalozzi never learned; he remained a most untidy man.

In the wintertime professional spinners and weavers came to the farm to teach the children how to make cloth. Goods were made by hand in those days, and the children thus learned a trade to follow when they grew up. Some of them became quite good at it; the sale of their finished work helped support the school.

Three hours each day were devoted to lessons. And these lessons, simple reading and writing and counting, were Pestalozzi's real challenge. His "family" came from homes in which the members knew nothing of books or numbers. To teach them at all was almost like teaching the blind to see or the deaf to hear.

But Pestalozzi had patience. Undoubtedly his difficulties at school helped him to understand the bewilderment of his pupils. To him no child was stupid. Some might be slower than others; some might be better at one thing than at another. All had God-given brains, if only one could awaken them. They must be taught in terms they could understand. He encouraged questions. And instead of learning by rote, he taught them to *think*.

He used no books. The children learned through their eyes and ears, their hands and minds. They learned to listen closely to notes of music; soon they were singing with gusto. They listened to the sounds of words and to the sounds of the letters that make up words. Soon, without even learning the alphabet by heart, they were spelling by ear. (Such spelling, called "phonetic," is easier in most foreign languages than in English; too many English words are spelled differently from the way they sound.)

Pestalozzi stirred their brains to the meanings of words. Even the smallest ones used their heads in answering such a very simple question as, "Is an apple tree a fruit tree or a forest tree?" or "What is oatmeal made of?" Then, asking questions themselves, they went on to learn about fruits, or oats, or whatever else "Papa" could persuade them to be interested in. They started learning arithmetic by measuring a plot of land for planting and by weighing the farm produce.

The children thrived. Pestalozzi did not. His enthusiasm carried him too far; he took in more and more waifs and strays until he had almost a hundred. To feed and clothe them he had to borrow money but found he could not pay it back. After five years he had to close down his school and part with his beloved "family."

There is no record of what became of them. Certainly they had a better chance in life for their stay at Neuhof.

STANZ

In teaching the children at Neuhof, Pestalozzi had learned a lot himself. He had puzzled out his own ways of awakening children's interest. And he had proved his belief that young people behave better when they are happy and encouraged. Alone on his farm he wrote about his ideas. In 1798 he had another chance to prove them.

Switzerland at this time had been caught up in the warring factions of the French Revolution. The town of Stanz on Lake Lucerne had defied the revolutionaries; French soldiers had burned down the town and killed its inhabitants. Its children were left without parents or shelter; they roamed the countryside like wild animals, begging, stealing, managing as best they could to keep alive. When government officials finally rounded them up they were a sorry lot. What to do with them? Pestalozzi applied for the job of caring for them, and the officials did not hesitate.

He was given a convent that had not been wholly burned and some funds for food, fuel, and blankets. He was also given a housekeeper—and seventy-three young savages to tame and teach.

He found his task much harder than with the Neuhof group. Those boys and girls had been merely ignorant; these were young hoodlums. While some were grateful and eager to learn, too many resented this change in their lives—which, after all, had been exciting, if uncomfortable. Pestalozzi understood.

"Man is good and desires to be good," he wrote. "If he is evil, it is because the way along which he was meant to follow has been blocked for him."

The ways of the Stanz orphans had certainly been blocked by horror and by the cruelty of hunger. Patiently, Pestalozzi tried to gain their trust.

"Everything done for them in their need, all the teaching they received, came directly from me," he wrote later. "My hand rested on their hand, my eye rested on their eye. My tears flowed with theirs, and I smiled with them. Their food was mine and their drink was mine. I slept in their midst; I was the last to go to bed at night, and the first to rise in the morning. I prayed with them, and taught them in bed before they went to sleep."

This all sounds somewhat sentimental. It was undoubtedly sincere. Yet, in spite of all his gentle efforts, "Papa" had to sometimes resort to a licking or two to keep order.

Silence in the classroom he insisted upon. His own voice was poor; he never could make it carry through clamor. And much of his teaching was by ear. As at Neuhof, there were no books; but neither were there any materials for spinning and weaving. It had been planned that the rescued children would cultivate the grounds around the old convent. However, the winter proved to be an unusually icy one, so that work on the grounds was impossible. All the more time for lessons.

Thus it was that boys and girls who had been living like young wolves found themselves sitting quietly in rows at six o'clock in the morning, repeating a prayer, singing a hymn, and listening to the sounds of syllables.

"Ab, eb, ib, ob, ub," they chorused. "Ad, ed, id, od, ud...," and went on to spell and even to write.

"Papa" Pestalozzi had worked out his own system of teaching writing. Just as he had broken down words into syllables, he broke letters into their parts: lines, arcs, hooks, and loops. His children practiced drawing these before attempting to draw a letter—a brand new idea in penmanship.

Arithmetic had always puzzled Pestalozzi. It was not until he had worked out for himself the relationships of numbers that they meant anything to him at all. So he worked out a way of making numbers understandable to his scholars. Using small pieces of wood, he taught them how to add and subtract before even trying to teach them how to write down the figures. This approach to arithmetic became famous through his use of it in his later school.

Although Pestalozzi's lessons sound quite elementary and obvious to us today, at the time they were quite new. Adolphe E. Meyer, a well-known professor of education, has said, "The modern elementary school was cradled in the tiny town of Stanz."

When, after a few months, the officials visited the school they were amazed. Not only had the little wild animals been tamed; they were apparently healthy, happy, and very smart at mental arithmetic! And they loved and trusted "Papa" Pestalozzi.

But before the year was out, the French soldiers returned to Stanz and demanded the old convent for a hospital. Again, Pestalozzi's school was disbanded.

YVERDON

By now "Papa" Pestalozzi's fame as a teacher was spreading. Other educators in Europe had been thinking and writing about improving children's dreary schools, but Pestalozzi alone had actually tried out his ideas and found them good. Young men who planned to be teachers came to him to learn the "new way." And in 1805 he acquired an old castle outside the Swiss town of Yverdon for his new school. Here he planned to train teachers, as well as to teach boys, according to his new ideas.

The school had a romantic setting. The castle, built some four hundred years previously by a duke called Charles the Bold, stood on the vine-covered shores of Lake Neuchâtel. Its four towers looked to the Alps and Mont Blanc on one side and, on the other, to the wide countryside flowing away toward France. The great towers and walls enclosed an inner courtyard, the former promenade of knights and ladies, which now served nicely as both shower room and field for prisoner's base. Narrow, winding stone steps reached from one floor to another; huge fireplaces heated the stony rooms, seven of which were converted into schoolrooms. The rest of the castle provided living quarters for "Papa" and his wife, 15 teachers, 180 boys, and more than 30 student teachers.

It was probably comfortable enough, as castles go—although one little boy named Freddie wept bitterly because it had no "parlor," that cozy room, heated by a gleaming tiled stove, which was the gathering place in every good Swiss home. And another small boy, who grew up to write affectionately of the school, admitted that he was shocked at the untidiness of the schoolroom—and of "Papa" Pestalozzi himself.

Pestalozzi was fifty-nine when he started Yverdon. But he had never outgrown the boy called "Harry Oddity." A new teacher described him as "an appalling sight, wearing an old gray overcoat; no waistcoat; a pair of breeches; and stockings falling down over his slippers—bushy black hair" that had not even started to gray. But the young teacher was soon won over, as were the boys, by Pestalozzi's spirit, if not his appearance.

Large as it was, the Yverdon school was still run like a family. The boys ranged from six to seventeen years of age. They came from all over the world: Germany, France, Russia, Italy, Spain, even America. It was not a free school; but "Papa" Pestalozzi, like Alcuin and Vittorino before him and many fine masters since, took in a number of boys whose parents could not pay. All tuition fees were kept in an unlocked box in Pestalozzi's study, available to all in need of cash. The student teachers were paid nothing beyond their board and keep; however, should they need money for a coat or a pair of shoes, they were told simply to go to the money box and help themselves. It seems that Pestalozzi, for all his concern over arithmetic, did not care for bookkeeping.

The teachers deserved any handouts they took, for they worked long, hard days. Pestalozzi's first principle was that the teacher must be the child's friend. To some teachers, the relationship must have seemed more like being the child's mother. They had to sleep in the same room with the boys, help the younger ones to bathe and dress, and be on hand at all times to answer any questions that might pop into the youngsters' heads. They sat with the boys at their lessons, learning Pestalozzi's ways of teaching. And between times they worked in the fields, for Pestalozzi's love of farming had its outlet at Yverdon. The school produced its own vegetables and fruits and dairy products. The teachers, too, cut and hauled the quantities of firewood used for cooking and for heating the great castle in winter.

The boys themselves were kept busy and well-fed. A five-thirty rising bell roused them from their beds in time to dress for their first lesson at six, after which they repaired to the courtyard for a good wash. The castle court had been equipped with a great pipe riddled with holes; as water was pumped through the pipe it spurted in jets from the holes, providing showers for the boys. Such outdoor baths, pleasant enough in summer, must have taken courage at seven o'clock on a winter's morning. But these boys were accustomed to a hardy life.

Clean and clothed again, the school now went indoors for prayers and a breakfast of hot soup. Lessons followed throughout the morning with a short break at ten, when those who were hungry could go to the housekeeper for a ration of bread and fruit. At noon came an hour of exercise and games: prisoner's base, or drill, or bathing in the lake in warm weather. At one o'clock all sat down to a hearty dinner of soup, meat, and vegetables. More lessons followed until half-past four, when fruit and cheese or bread and butter were laid out for the hungry. This snack a boy could take with him to eat where he pleased; his time was his own until six o'clock. Many boys had garden plots that they tended during this free time; others walked or played games or worked on some project in which they were interested. From six to eight came more lessons, ending in a supper of more soup and meat and vegetables.

This schedule appears today to include a great many hours

of lessons and a great deal of soup. But the soup, made of home-grown garden produce, was undoubtedly thick and good. And the lessons, as arranged by Pestalozzi, were often more like play than work.

To study geography, for instance, the boys went on voyages of discovery to the valley and surrounding countryside, observing and measuring as they went. They gathered clay at the riverbank and brought it back to school. Then, seated at a long table, they joined in making a relief map of their discoveries. Each boy in the group was responsible for a certain part of the map, which took several trips and much piling and molding of wet clay before it was finished. Only when it was done were they shown an actual relief map of the territory they had reproduced, so as to compare it with their own work.

Younger boys learned reading and spelling by means of Pestalozzi's method of chanting syllables. To write, they struggled with the same curves and pothooks as did the children at Neuhof and Stanz. But for arithmetic, instead of using slivers of wood, the master had now worked out a series of charts intended to explain the meaning of arithmetic in simple terms. Using the charts was rather like counting on one's fingers—provided one had several hundred fingers.

The first chart was used for problems in multiplication, such as: "If a man travels 3 miles in one hour, how far will he travel in 4 hours?"

To solve this knotty problem, a boy found the block with 3 marks in it, representing the miles traveled in 1 hour. Then he counted the marks in 4 of these hour blocks and came up with the answer of 12 miles. Thus he proved to himself that $3 \times 4 = 12$.

Chart II explained fractions. The top row of blocks represented whole units; the others were equally divided into parts.

"A boy had 4 oranges and divides them so as to give ½ orange to each of his friends. How many friends has he?"

To solve this, the student found the block which was divided

CHART NO. I

CHART NO. II

CHART NO. III

in half, to represent each orange. He then counted out 4 such boxes for his 4 oranges; and by counting up the spaces, found that the fortunate boy had 8 friends.

Chart III was used to multiply fractions. With this could be answered such questions as: "A boy having one third of an orange gave one third of that away. What part of the *whole* orange did he give away?"

The boy went to the third line of the chart, where the block represented his orange as divided into thirds. Then he turned to the right and found the block where those thirds were themselves divided into thirds. He now counted the spaces made by dividing thirds into thirds, found that there were nine, and concluded that the generous lad had given away one ninth of a whole orange.

It seems that by figuring out these charts, and making them up for themselves, the boys at Yverdon became very clever at arithmetic. Pestalozzi's charts became well known and were used by other schools as a basis for studying figures.

Geometry was another "do it yourself" subject. The boys worked at this with cardboard, making geometric planes and solids and figuring out the relationships of measurements. Some of them became remarkably good at it and held classes of their own in the town of Yverdon to instruct interested grownups!

Much time at Yverdon was spent in nature study. Each spring the teachers took groups of boys on field trips into the foothills of the Jura Mountains, the range dividing Switzerland from France. Even the smallest ones were invited on this strenuous trip. One small boy who had started school at the age of seven wrote later of the kindness of his teachers—how they heartened the stragglers with lumps of sugar dipped in brandy; and how, when the short legs of the younger ones began to ache, a cart was hired from a farmhouse to carry them the rest of the way. In the mountains the boys picnicked, sang Alpine songs, and gathered herbs and minerals for their collections. Afterward they gave oral or written accounts of their discoveries on the trip.

For the times, Yverdon offered an amazing variety of subjects. Boys could go in for languages—French, German, and Latin—and for music, drawing, gymnastics, bookbinding, even military drill. This last was a required subject—rather surprising at such a gentle school. But those were warlike days in Europe, and a knowledge of soldiering was only sensible.

The drill at Yverdon had its own imaginative flourishes. The boys not only marched with a flag and a band with a real drum, but wore homemade armor and carried homemade weapons as well. They held mock skirmishes in the countryside, with townsfolk and neighbors joining in the games. In the winter they built snow forts for their battles; there was always plenty of fine Swiss snow for ammunition.

Yverdon was a year-round boarding school. But at Christmas time there was such a series of festivities that the boys had no time to be homesick. A great fir tree was cut from the forest, hauled through the snow to the school, and decked in good German fashion with candles, gilded nuts, apples, and sweets. To many foreign boys, this was their first sight of a Christmas tree.

On New Year's Day the parents came to visit, bringing presents for their boys. The day began with a religious service; then came a fine feast and the exchange of presents. For weeks past the boys had been engaged in binding their best schoolwork into albums, which they now presented to their families—who undoubtedly glowed with pride over a pressed fern, a drawing of a cow, or a neat page of geometry. When darkness fell the whole school formed a torchlight procession and paraded through the town, singing and shouting blessings as they went.

The last and most elaborate festival was the celebration of Pestalozzi's birthday on January 12. The boys would turn the seven classrooms into miniature woodland scenes, bringing in moss, fir branches and ivy to form the settings, and making cottages and chapels, hills and distant views by means of cardboard and lighted transparencies. And to cap these scenic wonders, they would put on plays—episodes from Swiss history—which they had dramatized themselves as "surprises" for their master.

For twenty years Pestalozzi was suitably surprised by the offerings of his boys. What surprised him even more was the growing fame of his school throughout the world. Teachers who had studied under him carried his ideas to other countries. Reformers were taking a new interest in schools at this time; and not only schoolmasters, but nobles and princes came to look. And when the emperor of Austria awarded him a decoration for his contribution to learning, even the unworldly Pestalozzi could not help but be flattered. For a week he carried his medal with him, showing it off to all who would look. Then of course he mislaid it and forgot all about it.

For success did not change "Papa" Pestalozzi. All his life he remained a character—untidy, unbusinesslike, unfailingly kind. The story was told of him that once, on the way to town to visit the mayor, he gave a beggar the silver buckles from his shoes. Then, since his shoes would not stay on, he simply tied them with some wayside straw and went on his way. On his arrival at the mayor's palace he was promptly arrested as a suspicious character and held under guard until the mayor himself came forth and greeted his old friend with respectful apologies.

A statue of Pestalozzi stands today in the old town of Yverdon. The sculptor has tidied up his appearance. But he has caught, in the face and outstretched hand, the infinite gentleness of the man who was a friend to children.

Puritan Schools

The Praises of My Tongue
I offer to the Lord
That I was taught and learnt so young
To read his holy Word.

That I was taught to know
The Danger I was in
By Nature and by Practice too
A wretched slave to sin.

That I was led to see
I can do nothing well;
And whither shall a Sinner flee
To save himself from Hell.

—*The New England Primer*

The Puritans who came to settle in America were deeply pious.
They were also hard-working and very brave. It was for the
freedom to practice their own faith that they had dared the
perils of the Atlantic Ocean in sailing ships to take up life in a
country that was strange, often dangerous, and never comfortable. By 1640 some 20,000 of them were living in New
England and struggling with rocky soil, Indians, illness, and
the everyday needs of food, shelter, and warmth in a climate
far more rugged than they had ever known.

Puritan Schools

Puritan children were taught by their parents to fear God, to beware of the Devil, and to defend themselves. The law required that every boy between the ages of ten and sixteen learn the use of such weapons as small guns, half-pikes, and bows and arrows.

Book learning, however, was largely neglected. Though parents were supposed to teach their own young ones to read and write, it seems they were too busy with their daily toil to indulge in such frills. True, there were a few grammar schools scattered here and there where ambitious boys could study Latin; and there was Harvard College, founded in 1636 with an enrollment of twelve students, to prepare young men for the ministry. But most families were too poor and too busy for this kind of thing; and in 1647 the Massachusetts founders realized with horror that the great majority of young people were growing up without knowing how to read the Bible! So they enacted a law which has come down in history as "Ye Olde Deluder Satan Acte."

"It being one of the chief projects of that old deluder Satan to keep men from the knowledge of the Scriptures," the law explained, it was now required that every town of fifty families should support a teacher of reading and writing; while every town of a hundred families must support a grammar school "to fit youths for the University."

So it was the Devil, after all, who caused compulsory schooling. At any rate, historians claim that this law was the beginning of our American public-school system.

The Puritan school, however, was a very tiny ancestor of today's imposing school buildings. The schoolhouse was a one-room log cabin. Its only heat was from an open fireplace with a great chimney of stones daubed with clay, which not only carried off the smoke but let in the rain and snow. Firewood was supplied by parents, who hauled it by sledge to the schoolyard; and the schoolboys had the task of cutting it into log lengths and stoking the fireplace. Pupils whose parents were slow in providing their share of wood were made to sit farthest from the fire, back in corners so drafty that even all their layers of woolen clothing could not keep out the chill; and if this punishment failed, such children were dropped from the school. Often the wood was still green when it reached the hungry maw of the fireplace and sputtered viciously, filling the already dim room with smoke. The only light came from one or two small windows set high in the wall. For lack of glass, these were covered with oiled paper that could be removed in summer for better ventilation—for the cabin could be as hot in summer as it was drafty in winter. Its only furnishings were backless benches hewn from logs and a tall sloping desk and high stool for the teacher from which he could oversee his scholars.

Into this cheerless enclosure trooped the young Jonathans and Abigails of the day, in their gray homespun clothes with neat turned-down white collars. School began at seven o'clock on a summer morning and eight o'clock in winter and remained open throughout the year, with only a short holiday between the summer and winter sessions. The boys sat on one side of the room, the girls on the other. The school day, as in England, opened with prayers and closed with prayers, letting out at five in summer and four in winter. There was a break between eleven and one o'clock for dinner, chores, and perhaps a bit of play—although the Puritans frowned upon children's games as a waste of time. For the rest of the day, the boys and girls studied their alphabet, their Bible, and their duty to God and their parents.

For more than forty years such schoolbooks as there were came from England. The grammar schools used *Lily's Latin Grammar*; the elementary schools were limited to the Bible, a few hornbooks for the littlest ones, and perhaps a reader or speller printed in a type that would anguish the strongest eyesight. With these scarce materials the pupils—and the teachers —had to make do. Most of the learning was "by heart" anyway, from the spelling of syllables through the fearsome Puritan catechisms—those formal questions and answers which the

children had to know in order to save their souls. For the Puritans, unlike Pestalozzi, firmly believed that their babies were born wicked, and that their upbringing should be a stern battle with sin.

"What muſt become of you if you are wicked?" was one of the questions put to four-year-olds; and the tots were expected to answer promptly: "If I am wicked I ſhall be ſent down to everlaſting Fire in Hell among wicked and miſerable creatures."

And if this unhappy prospect failed to quell all sinful giggles and squirmings, the teacher had a more immediate weapon against Satan—the birch rod.

Writing, however, was taught earlier in America than in England. The settlers were a practical lot; and writing is, of course, necessary to any kind of business. Both boys and girls were taught to write down words and to figure enough to keep accounts. Writing was done with quill pens and homemade ink. Families made their ink by gathering the bark of the swamp maple, boiling it in an iron kettle until the brew was thick and black, then adding iron sulfate to make it indelible. This ink was an uneven and spluttery fluid at best, and given to freezing overnight in the cold of the deserted schoolhouse (one of the early morning duties in winter, along with stoking the fireplace and fanning the blaze, was to thaw out the ink).

Paper, too, was of poor quality, scarce, and valuable. To save it, schoolchildren practiced their writing on birch bark. In writing, as in reading, they made do with what they had.

But in 1690 the gloom of the schoolroom was lightened by a new book. A Mr. Benjamin Harris, an English writer and printer, had gotten into trouble in London for his religious views and had fled to America. In Boston he set up a shop selling "Coffee, Tea, and Chucaletto," with a printing press in the back room. Here he wrote and printed the first American schoolbook, *The New England Primer*.

It was a tiny book, measuring $3\frac{1}{2}$ by $4\frac{1}{2}$ inches. Its pages were of crude brownish paper bound between stout wooden covers. Its print was such as no doctor would allow today. But it had pictures! And its lessons were in rhyme! Moral as they were—for they were as stern and fearsome as any Puritan father could wish for—its alphabet jingles sang their way like Mother Goose into children's hearts.

In ADAM'S Fall	Proud Korah's troop
We ſinned all.	Was ſwallowed up.
The Deluge drown'd	XERXES did die.
The Earth around.	And so muſt I.
Elijah hid	While youth do cheer
By Ravens fed.	Death may be near.

When boys and girls had learned the alphabet, poring over the inky print, shivering deliciously over the frightful fate of Elijah, proud Korah, and King Xerxes, they went on to spell out lively verses such as this:

GOOD CHILDREN MUST

Fear God all day,	Love Christ alway,
Parents obey,	In secret pray,
No false thing say,	Mind little play,
By no sin stray,	Make no delay,

In doing good.

So welcome was *The New England Primer* that its sales spread through all the settled parts of the country. New York and the South bought the precious little volume from Boston, placing it beside the family Bible on the household shelf. Other printers brought out new editions, with slightly different rhymes and stories; sometimes they added a catechism for good measure. But the opening warning, "In ADAM'S Fall We ſinned all," remained unchanged through the years, a constant reminder to young folks to mend their ways.

District Schools

Reading and writing and 'rithmetic
Taught to the tune of a hickory stick . . .

As the New England population increased and the danger from Indians lessened, the huddled townsfolk spread out into their surrounding countryside, taming the land, building, and planting as they went. The single log-cabin school of the town could no longer take care of all the children, even with boys and girls taking turns at the winter and summer sessions. And many lived too far from the town, with no school buses to pick them up at the corner.

For a time some communities made out with a "moving school." The teacher went from one rural district to another, stopping at each one to teach there for a couple of months a year, or longer if the district could afford him.

But after the Revolution, the districts began to build their own schools.

They were humble enough little buildings, constructed long before the days of central heating, electric lights, airy schoolrooms, and gymnasiums. Even had such luxuries been thought of, it is doubtful that they would have been put into schools. Yankee country folk were poor as well as thrifty. The war had been costly, and many people who had no children of their own resented being taxed for the schooling of other folks' young'uns. Most district committeemen, however, bowed to the law, chose a bit of land that was good for nothing else, and built a one-room schoolhouse on it. They then hired a young man who could read and write, was willing to teach these arts for a few dollars a month, and was hefty enough to control the children. If he knew some arithmetic, so much the better. A good "arithmeticker" could always be sure of a teaching job— for about ten dollars a month.

This schoolhouse, as simple as it was, was an improvement over the old Puritan model. Rough logs were replaced by a wooden frame or clapboard, generally dressed with a coat of paint. Since red paint was the cheapest and most durable, schools were usually red. The building now had six or eight small windows set with real glass panes to let in the light. Its inner walls were covered with rough plaster, soon grayed by smoke from the fireplace. A sloping shelf, three feet above the floor, ran around three walls of the room, serving as a desk for the boys and girls seated before it. Behind them, toward the center of the room, sat the littlest ones who were still learning their A B Cs. The ends of the tots' benches were enclosed with wooden blocks for arms, so that their wrigglings would not shove the end pupils onto the floor.

Jutting into the room was the teacher's high desk and stool, from where he could watch for signs of disorder. He had to keep his wits about him, for between twenty and a hundred pupils of varying ages might be crowded into a room 30 feet square. A major part of his job was to keep discipline. To help him, he had a ruler for unruly knuckles and a "gad," a lithe 5-foot hickory sapling, with which to reach the farthest sinners without having to climb over the benches.

There is no reason to believe that these early schoolteachers were cruel or even particularly severe. But physical punish-

ments were considered healthy and necessary. "Spare the rod and spoil the child" was the motto. The teacher who did spare the rod was suspected by parents of not being a good teacher!

The winter term started on the Monday after the great New England festival of Thanksgiving. Strengthened by their feasts of turkey and pumpkin pies, the folk of the district spent the weekend "redding up" the schoolhouse: the men making carpentry and roof repairs, the women scrubbing the windows, floors, and wooden benches nicked with schoolboys' carvings. Firewood was stacked in the yard; the water bucket, with its unhygienic dipper, was placed in its corner near the door; the school Bible was dusted off and set on the master's desk. All was put in readiness for Monday morning.

The school day started at eight o'clock. Older boys and girls, however, took turns at coming early to haul in the wood, get that fire started, and sweep the schoolroom floor. The younger children were lucky if the damp, smoky wood had caught to a blaze before the arrival of the teacher—the signal for them to hang their hats and wraps in the entryway and take their places on the wooden benches.

Lessons started with Bible reading. This opening ceremony was the privilege of the first (most advanced) class. As each pupil was called upon he arose, climbed out of his seat, and made his way to a certain crack in the floor in front of the teacher's desk. There, "toeing the mark" as it was called, he bowed to the teacher, opened the Bible to the assigned page, and struggled through the ancient and beautiful language— while the small ones wriggled and the teacher made up quill pens.

Next came writing lessons. The ordeal meant as much manual labor for the teacher as for the scholars, for it was he who had to make or "mend" the pens, mix the ink, make up the copybooks, and set the copy for each child. Copybooks he made by folding sheets of paper into four, stitching them together in the middle, cutting the folded edges to form leaves, and ruling them with lines. At the top of each page he himself

wrote, in his best hand, the copy for the child to follow. For
the younger ones, the samples were merely lines, curves, and
"pothooks." But as a pupil's fist grew more adept at controlling
the sputtering goose-quill pen, he copied with beautiful swirls
and flourishes some moral proverb such as "Procrastination is
the Thief of Time." Each pupil daily was supposed to fill a
page in his copybook.

Because the different classes were all in one room, some
worked at their writing or sums while others toed the mark to
recite. The second and third classes had their turns at reading
from the Bible; the little ones recited from their primers or
spellers. If it was hard to keep one's mind on writing curlicues
or adding sums while others were chanting, "C, *A*, *T*, *cat*.
R, *A*, *T*, *rat*," well, there was always the ferrule or the gad to
help one to concentrate.

After a short recess at ten thirty, the whole school went in
for spelling. The spelling book, officially entitled *The Grammatical Institute*, was generally referred to as "Old Blueback"
because of the dull blue paper that covered its wooden binding.
This book had been prepared by Noah Webster, the author of
Webster's Dictionary. It started out with the statement that
"Language or speech is the utterance of articulate sounds or
voices, rendered significant by usage, for the expression and
communication of thought." And if this did not awe the children enough, there was a picture of Professor Webster himself
that, one critic wrote at the time, was "so ugly that it scares the
children from their lessons."

The book started with the usual "ab, eb, ib" syllables,
then progressed to words, sentences, paragraphs, and moral
matters.

"A good child will not lie, swear, nor steal," it proclaimed.
"He will be good at home, and ask to read his book; when he
gets up he will wash his hands and face clean; he will comb his
hair and make haste to school; he will not play by the way as
bad boys do.

"As for those boys and girls that mind not their books and

love not the church and school . . . they will come to some bad end, and must be whipt till they mend their ways."

Old Blueback also included a group of fables and a catechism. A favorite fable was the story of the rude boy who, when caught stealing apples, refused to come down from the tree. The old farmer begged in vain; then plucked some grass and threw it up at him, which, not unnaturally, only made the boy laugh. "So the old man," said the story, "pelted him heartily with stones, which soon made the young Chap hasten down from the tree and beg the old Man's pardon."

Moral

If good words and gentle means will not reclaim the wicked, they must be dealt with in a more severe manner.

Between such lessons the book offered many sentences of wise advice. Among others:

"Shut the gate and keep the hogs out of the yard."

"The chewing of tobacco is a useless custom."

"The love of whiskey has brought many a stout fellow to the whipping post."

"Large bushy whiskers require a good deal of nursing and training."

Quaint as it seems to us today, Webster's speller was a cherished volume in America's homes as well as its schools. It was the first book to lay down rules for correct spelling in a country that had never given much thought to such details. It started a craze for spelling bees in the schools and town halls of country districts, at which folk spelled each other down for prizes and glory. Undoubtedly many of the children, with the din of spelling at school still ringing in their ears, could outspell their elders and betters.

Arithmetic was still a formidable subject. In 1788 a scholar named Nicholas Pike published an arithmetic book that caught the attention of George Washington, who praised it highly. Fortunately for Mr. Pike's sales, the government passed a law the following year requiring that arithmetic be taught in all

American schools. Many would-be teachers must have wrestled with "Old Pike," with its rules for "Extraction of the Biquadrate Root," and "To find the Time of the Moon's Southing," and "The Proportions and Tonnage of Noah's Ark." But the district schools did not trouble to solve such mysteries. Arithmetic was limited to addition, subtraction, multiplication, and division. The teacher set the sums in the children's handmade exercise books, to be worked out in small, neat figures so as not to waste precious paper.

Fortunate were the boys and girls who owned slates on which to practice their writing and arithmetic. The use of slates first started in Vermont, the home of slate quarries, where passing children could gather such fragments as tempted them. Soon merchants were cutting pieces of slate to shape, setting them in wooden frames, and selling them for the use of schoolchildren. Parents or teachers could make chalk pencils by this recipe:

> 1 lb. of wheat flour
> 5 lbs. of Paris white
> Wet with water and knead well. To roll, two boards are needed, one to roll them on, the other to roll them with. Experienced hand will make 150 in an hour.

Slates, however, were expensive; they cost about forty-four cents—a large sum for many rural folk; and a broken slate was a real tragedy. Abraham Lincoln, we are told, did not even own one. He worked his sums with charcoal on the back of a wooden spade, whittling away its surface to make a fresh "page."

Money was scarce in the country districts of New England. Many things were bought by trading: sacks of ground meal in exchange for shoes, or hours of work as payment for sawed wood. It was hard for many people to pay their share of the teacher's salary, small as it was. To save expenses, families took turns at boarding the teacher for a week or two at a time. Youngsters in a household were warned to practice their best behavior as the time approached for putting up their teacher.

They need not have worried. The schoolteacher, in most

cases, was not much more than a lad himself. Most often he was a youth in his teens, big and strong enough to keep discipline, whose object in teaching school was to earn money toward his own secondary schooling. Often he eked out his salary of ten, or at the most twelve, dollars a month by helping farmers in their fields. His pupils were surprised to find that their stern master, having locked his rod behind in the schoolhouse at evening, became a fun-loving elder brother, ready with tricks and games and a lullaby for the baby.

But boarding around was not always comfortable for a teacher. Often he must have been homesick for his own family. And his Yankee hosts, with large families to feed, were very thrifty. One young teacher gave an account of his week's board with the B—— family:

The household consisted of Mr. B—— and his wife, a daughter, four boys, a dog, and two cats. To prepare for their guest the B——s had killed and roasted a gander—which, the teacher wrote, "from its size, the thickness of skin and other venerable appearances, . . . must have been one of the first settlers of Vermont." He was able, however, to chew a little of the breast. For supper that night he was served cold gander and potatoes. Tuesday's breakfast was again cold gander, with "swamp tea" and nut cake—"the latter some consolation." Tuesday dinner, "the legs etc. of the gander done up warm— one nearly despatched. Supper—the other leg etc. cold." After which, on going to bed, he dreamed he was a mud turtle on its back, unable to turn over. Wednesday, "Cold gander for breakfast; complained of sickness and could eat nothing. Dinner— wings etc. of the gander warmed up; did my best to destroy them for fear they should be left for supper. . . . Supper—hot Johnnycake; felt greatly revived . . . went to bed for a good night's rest; disappointed; very cool night and couldn't keep warm; got up and stopped the broken window with my coat and vest; no use; froze the tip of my nose and one ear before morning. . . . Thursday:—Cold gander again; much discouraged to see the gander not half gone; went visiting for dinner and supper." He stayed away for the night and the morrow's breakfast, returning to the B—— family in time for a dinner of "cold gander and potatoes—the latter very good; ate them and went to school quite contented." Supper that night was "cold gander and no potatoes, bread heavy and dry; had the headache and couldn't eat." Saturday breakfast was "cold gander and hot Indian Johnnycake; did very well. Dinner—cold gander again; didn't keep school this afternoon; weighed and found I had lost six pounds the last week; grew alarmed; had a talk with Mr. B—— and concluded I had boarded out his share."

But probably all households were not so economical, nor their geese so tough, as Mr. B——'s.

The little district schools continued in America for many years. As time went by, stoves replaced fireplaces; pencils and writing tablets came into use; new schoolbooks were printed; and history and geography were added to the program.

Women became accepted as schoolteachers. At first they only taught the summer sessions, which, in some districts, were reserved for girls and very young boys. But as teaching became a real profession, more women went into it seriously and took on the task of teaching elementary school to children of all ages in the one-room district school.

Many adults can remember their early school days as trips through autumn leaves, or through the quiet magic of snow, or through the tantalizing damp greens of spring to the little schoolhouse where Miss —— stood awaiting the daily battles with the blackboard and the primer; or the sleepy, late spring days when, as the sun grew hot on the roof, she would miraculously decide on a trip to the pond to study nature.

Since schools have become large and central, with playgrounds and auditoriums and modern equipment to help with lessons, and buses to carry the pupils to and fro, the district schools have mostly been deserted. But there are still some rural parts of America where the school bell rings and the children make their way—running or loitering, depending on the weather—to the little red schoolhouse down the road.

American Academies

As for me, I study 13 hours every day, 6 devoted to Latin, the rest to chemistry and kindred subjects.

—Letter from a schoolboy at
Phillips Academy, Andover

By the 1800s the world's storehouse of knowledge was filling rapidly. Beyond reading, writing, arithmetic, and studies of the classics and the Scriptures, there were exciting new fields of learning. Men's eager minds had made discoveries in physics and chemistry, botany and geography, mathematics and history. But knowledge, like food, is not of much use to mankind if it is kept locked up. Before the days of free high schools, how could America's young people find out about these things?

Academies sprang up throughout the states. They were not free, but they did offer schooling beyond that provided by the town or district schools. Usually they were endowed—that is, partly supported by public-spirited men of wealth, and sometimes by town funds.

These schools proved to be immensely popular. By 1840 there were a hundred of them in Massachusetts alone. Each fall, throngs of young people who could afford the fee—and many who could not but hoped for a scholarship—set out for one or another of the "academy towns." Since the academy buildings were small, fitted with only a limited number of bedrooms, the majority of students were prepared to board in houses throughout the town in order to attend the classes.

By coach and by boat they came, on horseback and on foot, to reach their school. One youth from Providence, Rhode Island, walked 60 miles to Phillips Academy at Andover, Massachusetts, to apply for a scholarship—which, fortunately, he was granted. Another lad is said to have walked all the way from Mississippi. Perhaps he thumbed some rides on the way; even so, his trip was strenuous. When he finally reached Andover he was so tired and dirty that he did not dare present himself, but hid in the woods, where he was discovered trying to control his sobs of weariness and triumph.

The academy at Andover, the earliest and certainly one of the finest in New England, was particularly generous to ambitious boys. Samuel Phillips, its founder, was a wealthy man with a great interest in education. While the usual age for entering Phillips Academy was ten, many students were much older by the time they got the chance to go away to school. The youth who wrote that he studied for thirteen hours every day was eighteen when he reached Phillips; he had graduated from his local grammar school and worked four years in a plow factory before earning enough money to pay for the academy courses in chemistry which he needed to become a doctor. And the boy who walked from Providence had already been apprenticed to a tanner and had saved up a little money before setting out for Andover. He was granted the cost of his room and board—$1.25 a week—and was allowed to work out his tuition fees.

A boy who thus worked his way through the academy was called a "scholar of the house." His position was much respected, even though his chores were menial. His duties were to ring bells, sweep floors, haul wood, make up the fires, and so on. It was hard work, especially if he boarded some distance from the academy.

Households that boarded students were specially licensed by the school. The approved families had to promise to hold prayers night and morning, exact good manners and obedience from their boarders, and report any misbehavior to the academy. They were inspected at intervals by the trustees to be certain that all was in order: no late hours, no untidiness, no skipping of the prayer of "grace before meat." The usual fee to board a student was $1.25 or $1.50 a week—a good deal more money then than it is today.

Andover's earliest schoolroom was furnished with tiers of seats rising up on either side of a broad center aisle. It was heated by a great "Russian stove," an ornate porcelain affair that stood out in the room and consumed endless chunks of wood. "I rise early, breakfast by candlelight, hike to the Academy and make a fire by sunrise," wrote the scholar from Providence; and during the day he cut and hauled wood for three fires "which consume the fuel almost as fast as it is prepared."

In 1827 this schoolroom proudly acquired a blackboard. It was made of simple wooden boards painted black, and it covered one wall of the room. This novelty proved to be most useful for showing the correct spellings of words and for the working out of problems in arithmetic; other schools soon followed suit.

The boys prepared their lessons seated at a long table in the "study room." But as the number of students increased, the study table became uncomfortably crowded. In the 1830s when Andover added its "commons" or dormitories, students of "orderly deportment and serious habits" were now allowed to study in their own rooms.

Each room had its fireplace and a whale-oil lamp for light. Frugal boys who wished to save the price of their meals in the school dining room could use their fireplaces to cook their own meals. The results were scarcely a well-balanced diet. But those were days before canned goods and frozen foods; boys bought what supplies they could get and prepared them as best they could. One boy described his meals in a letter to his family:

MONDAY: hasty pudding [boiled cornmeal] and molasses for breakfast; cold hasty pudding and milk for both dinner and supper, with crackers to top off with.

TUESDAY: roasted potatoes with butter for breakfast; wheat and butter for dinner; warm Indian cake [corn bread] and butter for supper.

WEDNESDAY: boiled potatoes and butter for breakfast: bread and butter for dinner; warm Indian cake for supper.

The meals served at school were not much more luxurious. At Andover the breakfast was bread and butter; dinner, "bread without butter, potatoes, and sometimes corned pig and what is esteemed 'fishes' eyeballs' [undoubtedly tapioca pudding], India rubber, starch, and various other kinds of puddings."

Only at a very expensive school, costing three hundred dollars a year, did they serve bread and butter, baked apples, coffee, and milk for breakfast; and for dinner and supper meats, vegetables in season, and puddings. Those school puddings!—always of the "fishes' eyeballs" and "India rubber" varieties, intended to fill the bellies of schoolboys as they dreamed of the pies and preserves at home.

The principal of an academy was called the preceptor. Students had to rise when he entered the room, bow when he spoke to them, and always address him as "Sir." Such politeness was known as "making one's manners"; and manners were an important part of an academic education. The young scholars had to make their manners to teachers, ministers, parents; even to doff their caps to strangers on the street. Lapses in manners, like other misdeeds, were reported to the preceptor, who decided upon a suitable punishment.

Discipline was vigilant. But the preceptors do not seem to have been particularly harsh—at least compared to those in English boarding schools. Stories of American school life do not emphasize the fearful, flogging schoolmasters such as are found in the novels of Dickens. Some preceptors, no doubt, were ready with the birch rod; others had their preferred methods of discipline, ranging from heart-to-heart talks with the culprits to classroom humiliations. One Andover preceptor punished whisperers by putting a bit in their mouths, and restless squirmers by strapping horses' blinders to their temples!

Most punishments, however, took the practical Yankee form of fines. Deerfield Academy, one of the earliest and best schools, listed its rules and the cost of breaking them like items at a supermarket:

For absence from Sunday meeting, Fast Day, or Thanksgiving $1.

For playing cards, backgammon, or checkers in the building $1.

and so on, down to the less expensive crimes:

For playing ball near the academy 6¢
For absence from 5 AM prayers 4¢
For being late for prayers 2¢

The use of books from the school library had its financial perils. An ink blot on a page cost six cents, as did a drop of candle grease; a mark or scratch was two cents; while the price of a torn page was six cents an inch.

But the academy school day did not leave much time for getting into mischief. It started with prayers, held in most schools at seven thirty or eight, by which time many of the boys had already been up for several hours. The lad from Providence wrote home: "My rising hour is 5 o'clock, yet I very often get up before that hour. . . . I go to breakfast at 6 o'clock, commence studying immediately afterward."

Another youth who was a working scholar wrote: "Rise in the morning about 5:30 o'clock; build two fires (probably more when it is colder), work around the barn, milk one cow,

take care of the horses and saw wood until 7:30 when I eat my breakfast . . . then, if a man has stopped here over night, he usually starts away about this time, I put his horse in [into harness] etc. if not, I prepare for school and look over my lesson till 8:30 when I attend prayers at the Academy."

Classes and study periods went on until noon, with a twenty-minute recess at ten. After the noonday dinner, recitations and study were resumed until five, when there was another period of prayer.

The assortment of studies over which the boys pored by those fishy-smelling lamps was considered most advanced. Latin, of course, was fundamental; it was still the language of learning. Like their English cousins, academy boys grappled with the current textbook, *Cheever's Latin Accidence*, a dry and dreary volume that gave fifty-eight pages of grammar rules before it permitted a line of reading. But English grammar, too, was drilled into the boys' ears, and with good reason; many Yankee errors in speaking and writing had crept into American speech. The young gentlemen not only learned all about the parts of speech, but were trained to say *afraid* instead of *afeared*, *chimney* instead of *chimbley*, *cucumber* instead of *cowcumber*, *potatoes* for *taters*, and *umbrella* for *umberiller*.

Handwriting was another basic subject. Most academies had a special master for teaching this art. By 1832 steel pens were being used; they were more manageable than the old goose quills and gave rise to the fancy curves and swirls of the elegant writer, the mark of an educated man.

But beyond these accomplishments, the academies also offered such exciting subjects as arithmetic and geometry, geography and history, and the sciences of "natural philosophy" (simple physics), botany, astronomy, geology, and chemistry. As the sciences became popular with the students, the schools vied with each other in providing scientific equipment. Where at first a pair of globes, inaccurate and expensive, had been all that a schoolroom could offer, by 1849 the better academies could boast of a microscope—that instrument which Martin

Luther had accused of housing the Devil!—an air pump, a thermometer, an orrery (a miniature planetarium), measuring instruments, and even an "electric machine"!

New schoolbooks came off the presses, lively with pictures. Colburn's *First Lessons in Intellectual Arithmetic on the Plan of Pestalozzi*, with its boxes of lines like straws to be counted, gave way to Barnard's *Treatise on Arithmetic*, which had rows of birds and boys and stagecoaches to add and subtract. While younger boys learned about numbers by figuring these pictures, the more advanced were given such fascinating problems as the following:

> Adonibezek said, 3 score and 10 kings, having their thumbs and their great toes cut off, gather their meat under my table (Judges 1:7); how many toes and thumbs did Adonibezek cut off?

Geography books now had maps to bring them to life. The maps were not very accurate; the western part of America beyond the "Stony Mountains" was still a vague and uncharted territory. And the "facts" that the boys learned from their geography books make odd reading today. *Adam's Geography*, published in 1818, explains that:

> A MOUNTAIN is a vast protuberance of the earth.
>
> *Europe* is distinguished for its learning, politeness, government, and laws; for the industry of its inhabitants, and the temperature of its climate.
>
> *The White Mountains* are the highest not only in New Hampshire, but in the United States.
>
> Beer is the common drink of the inhabitants of *New York State*. The forests abound with bears, wolves, deer and elks.
>
> Many of the towns and plantations in *Maine* are destitute of any settled minister. Missionaries sent among them have been affectionately received.

By 1833 geographers had been doing their best to explore the rest of the country but had been having difficulty with the roads:

In the sandy, alluvial country of the Atlantic coast from New York to Florida, the roads are heavy, and not easily improved. The scattered state of population has prevented much attention to the roads, in the states south of Maryland; and frequent impediments are presented by the want of bridges and causeways, over the streams and marshes.

In the Western States, during the wet season, many roads are scarcely passable for wheel carriages. . . . The small streams are so variable that most of them can be forded during the dry seasons, and bridges are rarely built. [*Woodbridge's Universal Geography*]

But, promised the book, there was hope for a miraculous improvement in western travel:

A plan has recently been invented for constructing roads with iron bars, or railways, on which the wheels of carriages run so easily that they may be drawn from 15 to 30 miles an hour, by means of locomotive engines.

The promise came true. *Peter Parley's Geography* of 1837 says of railroads: "They are found so useful that, for carrying passengers from one place to another, they have, on many routes, taken the place of stage-coaches."

The history books, to our eyes, were also quaint. They mixed Biblical legends with historical facts; Adam and Eve were as actual as Solon of Athens. And *A History of the United States* by Noah Webster himself, that stickler for accuracy, traced our ancestors "from the dispersion at Babel to their migration to America."

American history was more detailed than European, since more was known of it. History books offered lively and boastful accounts of the settlers' troubles with Indians, of the Boston Tea Party, and of the Revolution.

"Our ancestors combined a practical religion with the most scrupulous morals," states Butler's *A History of the United States*, "which laid the foundation for a set of customs and habits, that operated upon society more forcibly, if possible, than the laws, and gave a peculiar force and energy to their civil codes. Under such a system, industry and frugality, patience and perseverance, magnanimity and valor, with a practical display of all the moral virtues, formed the characters of the first settlers of New England."

Smug as it was, such "lofty language," as it was called, was greatly admired in academy days. The young were urged, in their writings, to use as many syllables and commas as possible, and to talk in stilted sentences. A reader of 1807 even makes a joke of it in the following dialogue between an angry father and his academy-bred son:

OLD T.:   Ay, ay, Len, you must be chained in a dark room and fed on bread and water—O the Mackademy!

LEANDER: You may arraign me, Sir, with impunity for faults which I in some instances have been guilty of—but my improvements in the liberal arts and sciences, have been, I believe, equal to most of my standing, and I am confident, Sir, that I have asserted nothing but what is consistent with the philosophy of our times.

OLD T.:   Your dosolophys may go to Beelzebub, and you may go with them, Sir . . .

Declamation was a favorite subject. It taught not only lofty language but persuasive tones and gestures to go with it. At least one afternoon a week was given over to its practice. Boys learned by heart recitations suitable to their ages—from the immortal "You'd scarce expect one of my age/To speak in public on the stage . . ." to long classical and political speeches. Certain hard-and-fast rules governed proper recitation. In Lovell's *The Young Speaker*, published in 1844, the young orator was taught to approach the edge of the platform "with a gentle but assured step . . . a little of the right of centre, then pausing for a moment, he casts his eyes with a diffident respect over the audience." He had to then go through the correct motions of left foot, right foot, toe, heel, and shifting of his weight for his opening bow. "In this posture the body is kept for an instant; he then rises slowly to an erect attitude, and is ready to commence speaking." His speech, of course, was adorned with appropriate dramatic gestures.

Another popular subject was debating. Boys were divided into two teams to argue such weighty topics as votes for women, or whether novels should be allowed in school libraries, or whether the Louisiana Purchase had beeen worthwhile! These debates, too, were carried on in "lofty language" and fine oratorical style, and were undoubtedly good training for public speaking. But they had another use: a good debater, to persuade his audience, had to have not only strong arguments but a thorough knowledge of his subject. In their search for facts to back up their arguments some of the debating clubs, chipping in their own funds, collected quite impressive libraries for the use of their members.

Organized athletics had not yet come into fashion in this country. We can trust, however, that where there were boys there were ball games (as witness the fine of six cents for playing ball near the school). But New England no longer held the Puritan belief that play was a wicked waste of time; and there were fields at a safe distance from the school's glass windows where boys could play without punishment. Those who had time could kick a football or have a game of rounders (an old English game not unlike baseball). But sports, as such, were not part of the school curriculum. Schools, it was felt, were for learning.

And how proud were the towns of their temples of learning! Each year an academy exhibition was held, and a holiday was proclaimed throughout the district so that people might attend.

The great event took place in either a church or the town hall. The town band accompanied the school as it marched in solemn parade, with the trustees at the head followed by distinguished guests, then the teachers, then the students in order of their classes. Finally marched the audience, crowding in as best it could to admire the accomplishments of those clever academy boys.

The exhibition programs were impressive. Between bursts of music from the band, the younger boys piped their poems; the older ones debated, orated, and delivered truly awe-inspiring samples of their learned translations. One Andover boy amazed his audience with Webster's *Bunker Hill Oration* turned into Latin. Another gave Pitt's *Speech on the American Colonies* in Greek. Two others gave their Greek translation of a dialogue from Shakespeare.

Sometimes the audience was even treated to a play depicting some glorious incident in history. And occasionally, in some broad-minded communities, girls from a neighboring female seminary were allowed to take part—although the old folks blustered and wrote to the papers protesting such unseemly behavior.

Female Seminaries

Do you not know, child, that God is more pleased when his children look neat than when they don't?

—Miss ZILPAH GRANT, headmistress,
Ipswich Female Academy

For now girls, too, were going to academies.

In colonial days there had been little or no schooling of girls. Those early laws requiring that children be taught to read and write went on to explain that by "children" the law of course meant boys. Little girls might attend a special summer session at the town elementary school; or go to a private dame school; or, if they were wealthy, go to a "finishing school" where they learned to dance and read and paint in watercolors. But mostly they stayed at home and learned to bake and sew and be useful helpmeets to the menfolk.

Meanwhile, they learned their letters by stitching them on squares of linen called "samplers." First came the capitals, then the small letters and the numerals, then a neat and pious verse. The sampler was bordered by a charming pattern of flowers, birds, fruits, perhaps a house and a tree, all worked in bright stitches. The child then sewed her name, age, and the date for posterity; and the finished sampler was framed and hung in the parlor as proof of the cleverness of little Hannah or Amanda.

After the Revolution, however, girls began to be taken more seriously. Bright women as well as men were needed to build the new Republic. Girls now attended the district schools; and it was even felt they might be allowed some further learning. Dr. Benjamin Rush, a signer of the Declaration of Independence, spoke out strongly for educating girls, if only to prepare them to be better wives and mothers.

"To be mistress of a family is one of the great ends of a woman's being," he pointed out, and went on to prescribe her suitable studies. She should know the English language thoroughly as to its reading, spelling, and grammar, and should be able to write it down in a fair and legible hand. She should also learn arithmetic and bookkeeping "in order to qualify her for the duties which await her in this country." And she ought to know at least enough geography and history to make her "an agreeable companion to a sensible man." In addition, he advised, she should certainly study enough astronomy and physics to be able to laugh at superstitions and old wives' tales. Nor should she neglect the womanly pursuits of religious devotions, sweet singing, and graceful dancing—the latter an exercise that he considered both healthy and attractive.

But these subjects, said Dr. Rush firmly, were enough. To play an instrument was a useless frill for a girl in this hardworking country—besides, it was too expensive. French and drawing were a waste of time. American girls, he warned, could not hope to have servants to wait upon them like their English cousins, and so would not have the leisure in which to draw pictures or to talk French!

Whether or not New England parents heeded Dr. Rush, who lived in far-off Pennsylvania, they began sending their daughters to school.

Some of the early academies, such as Deerfield, Massachusetts, took in girls as well as boys. Their lives, however, were kept quite separate. The girls went into the building by sep-

arate entrances and climbed separate stairs to the separate floors where their classes were held. Their playground was separated by a high board fence. Only at prayers and meals did they see the boys. Boys and girls were not allowed to meet "within or outside of the school walls, nor walk nor ride nor visit together under penalty of $1"—a discouraging price for a chat with a member of the opposite sex.

Before long female academies, or female seminaries as they were usually called, were flourishing throughout New England. Like the boys' academies, they were boarding schools that girls could attend for one, two, or three years to get some of the knowledge now offered to their brothers.

Girls started in at an academy at various ages. Some girls were sent at seven; others had been through district school; some, like many of the boys, had even taught school before they got their chance at the academy. And while they did not chop wood or milk cows, there were scholarships and jobs as assistants to help those who couldn't pay the full fee.

Many girls, like the boys, traveled far to get to school—and travel, in those days, was a rigorous business. One Vermont girl rode horseback the 150 miles to Litchfield Academy in Connecticut. Since her horse could not very well carry her trunk, she had to have her wardrobe made at Litchfield. A New York girl at the same school described her journey home for the holidays. She and her friends climbed into the stagecoach at ten in the morning and arrived at New Haven at eight that evening, where they boarded a sailing ship for New York. But there was no wind that night or the next day, so they could not sail. The young ladies improved their time by viewing New Haven, until the captain sent for them to come aboard in time for an evening breeze which carried them to New York, where they finally docked at nine o'clock the next morning. It had taken them forty-seven hours to traverse a distance that by car is seventy miles!

When railroads came in, the journeys were, of course, easier.

Still, railroads were few and slow; for many years they puffed along at the breathtaking speed of fifteen miles an hour.

Upon their arrival at school, the girls would pack away their best bonnets and shawls, hang up their simpler school frocks in readiness, and settle down to academy life. Like the boys, most of them boarded in town under the watchful eyes of "approved" families. Early to bed and early to rise was the rule, with prayer and Bible reading at both ends of the day. Next in importance to piety—and so close as to seem almost a part of it—came "decorum." This meant not only good manners, proper curtsys, and low, pleasant speaking voices, but neatness in dress and habits. Litchfield girls were asked to examine their souls for faults at the end of each day:

"Have you been neat in your chamber?" "Combed your hair?" "Cleaned your teeth?" "Been present at table?" "At family prayers?" and so on through a long list of such ladylike requirements.

"Every hour during the week must be fully occupied in either useful employments or necessary recreation," cautioned the rules. "Two hours a day must be devoted to close study. . . . The ladies where you board must mention if you do not study your two hours each day."

Strict order was kept in the classroom. "Whispering," said Miss Zilpah Grant of Ipswich, "is the beginning of all school trouble," and forbade it absolutely. Hartford Female Academy ruled that "no young lady during school hours in any part of the building may communicate ideas to another by the mouth, by the fingers, or by writing without leave."

In this solemn silence the young ladies bent their serious combed heads to study. Even their books wore trim dresses sewed on by their owners. Schoolbooks of the time were bound in covers of thin wood pasted over with blue or brown paper, but the female scholars preferred to slip-cover them in bright calico. "Thumb papers" were another tidy fashion: squares of some strong, bright-colored paper were folded to form triangular pockets, attached to the book by a cord, and slipped over the lower corner of an open page to protect it from the marks of studious thumbs.

Girls were not expected to go in for Latin and Greek. But their other courses were somewhat diluted versions of those the boys took. English grammar was heavily stressed; correct grammar was almost as important for a young lady as correct behavior. Academy girls—from various backgrounds with, no doubt, various American dialects—had to know their grammar inside out.

The younger scholars had picture books to help them with the parts of speech. Older girls used a grammar specially prepared for them by schoolmaster Caleb Bingham:

THE YOUNG LADY'S ACCIDENCE:
or a short and easy Introduction to English Grammar,
Designed principally for the use of young Learners,
more especially for those of the FAIR SEX,
though proper for either.

Perhaps the compliment of being called "the Fair Sex" helped the girls to memorize its sixty pages of grammatical rules. As soon as they had conquered these, they were given such exercises as parsing the first sentence of *Paradise Lost*—which is sixteen lines long.

Like the boys, the girls studied history and geography, chemistry and "natural philosophy" (simple physics). These latter formidable subjects were made more alluring to girls by two cozy textbooks prepared for them by Mrs. Jane Marcet and entitled *Conversations on Chemistry* and *Conversations on Natural Philosophy*. A young girl named Emily, plagued by the endless questions of her young sister Sophie, comes to Mrs. B. for help. Mrs. B. agrees to instruct Emily, and the books are in the form of dialogues such as this:

*Now that you are acquainted with the attraction of cohesion, I must endeavor to explain to you that of *gravitation*, which is a modification of the same power; the first is perceptible only in very minute particles, and at very small distances; the other acts on the largest bodies, and extends to many distances.

EMILY: You astonish me: surely you do not mean to say that large bodies attract each other.

MRS. B.: Indeed I do: let us take for example one of the largest bodies in nature [the earth] . . .

In this way, Mrs. B. goes on to explain the laws of gravity, motion, optics, astronomy and the planets, and so on to "Galvinism or Voltaic Electricity," ending up with the unsolved mystery of the electric eel.

But moral philosophy was far and away the girls' most important study. It was their thorough grounding in this subject that set them above their less-educated sisters. For the headmistresses had other aims for their pupils than to become a mere "agreeable companion to a sensible man." Female education had the bit in its teeth; those girls were to go forth and enlighten the world. They must spread not only the words of religion, but such everyday virtues as right living, right thinking, and the right uses of brains.

A basic textbook for moral philosophy was Isaac Watts's *On the Improvement of the Mind*, usually known as *Watts on the Mind*. The book was actually written for boys who were planning to become ministers, but the girls studied it for its high moral values.

"Deeply possess your mind with the vast importance of good judgment," Dr. Watts began his book, "and the rich and inestimable advantages of right reasoning." He went on for twenty-two chapters on such topics as how to improve one's powers of observation, how to judge books, and which subjects of study were worthy of Christian attention. He approved of the natural sciences as rousing a due appreciation of the works of the Creator. He even had kind words for arithmetic: to solve a tricky problem in numbers, he advised, was a better p⸗ me for youth than gaming and drinking!

Girls—perhaps because they did not need su   fenses

against gambling and drinking—did not go very deeply into mathematics. Most academies carried them through "computing interest," but that was all. Girls concentrated more on thinking deep thoughts and writing them down.

Elegant composition was another specialty of the female seminary. Weekly letters to families had first to be submitted to teachers for approval of contents and corrections in spelling. And every two weeks the young ladies had to hand in a two-hundred-word essay on some solemn subject such as pride, prejudice, or intellectual culture. Little Harriet Beecher, who would one day be Mrs. Harriet Beecher Stowe, author of *Uncle Tom's Cabin*, wrote a fine essay on "The Difference between the Natural and Moral Sublime" at the age of nine.

The handwriting of the essays was as dressy as the wording. A visiting teacher came once or twice a week to help the scholars with the loops and swirls of ladylike script. French and music, too, were usually taught by visiting teachers.

With no Latin or Greek to fret over, the girls had time for the more feminine accomplishments of drawing, painting with watercolors, and needlework. These pretty skills, however, were used to dress up more serious matters. For geography, for instance, the girls drew charming maps and then painted them in delicate colors. Some clever needlewomen worked their maps in embroidery—in stitches more accurate than the map itself. And for botany, the favorite science, they could draw and paint and embroider flowers to their hearts' content. As they worked at these handicrafts, their preceptress read aloud from some uplifting book "to improve their language and sentiments; and to inculcate some of the more important principles of piety and virtue."

But academy life was not all solemn. Those girls had good times. The old belief that girls were made of spun glass was passing away. Physical exercise was encouraged; a student got extra good marks for taking some exercise before breakfast. And during recess and after class hours, the young ladies were urged to skip rope, toss beanbags, and play on swings and seesaws in the open air. Fresh air was beginning to come into fashion; New England's countryside provided plenty of it.

There were walks in the country to "observe nature," during which the girls were allowed to run and chat as well as observe. There were boat rides on the pond or river, and excursions by coach to see the sights of other towns. When railroads came into being, groups of young ladies were given the new and amazing experience of a ride "in the cars." And a New England winter could always promise sleigh rides, all jingling bells and tingling cheeks, followed by hot possets around the schoolroom stove.

Best of all, in early spring came "sugaring off" parties. With the snow still on the ground, workers at the neighboring sugar camp had tapped the maple trees and set their sap to boil in iron cauldrons, simmering it for days over a huge log fire. When the syrup came to the thickening point, folk were invited to come and eat their fill. The thick, hot syrup was poured onto clean snow, which immediately cooled it to a delicious sort of caramel candy. The girls from the female seminary were invited on a special night, which was the high spot of the sugarbush season.

Female schools, too, had their exhibitions. The young ladies did not orate in Greek and Latin, but they sang prettily, recited poetry, and showed samples of their best maps, essays, and embroidery. Sometimes they even put on a play, most often based on some Biblical story, and made their own costumes, and forgot their lines, and giggled, and were forgiven by their admiring audience.

Graduation from an academy was a more final step for the girls than for the boys. Youths, when they finished their courses, received "certificates" that enabled them, if they wished, to go on to college. But for the girls, graduation marked the end of their formal schooling. They were given "diplomas"—as impressive in those days as university degrees today. At Litchfield Academy the diplomas were engraved on white silk edged in blue. The young girl graduates wore white and dabbed damp handkerchiefs to reddened eyes. For it was considered only fitting that young ladies should weep at the prospect of leaving their sheltered halls to take on their responsibilities in the great outside world.

And seminary girls lived up to their education. Many became the wives of ministers, professors, or missionaries and helped their husbands in these fields. So many were chosen as brides by men of the cloth that their schools were dubbed "ministers' rib factories."

But many of the girl graduates went in for teaching. They carried the lamps of both natural and moral philosophy throughout the young nation. For not only in New England was their knowledge appreciated; the West was being settled and was crying out for teachers for its children. And the more courageous among the seminary graduates answered the call —all young and tremulous and filled with high ideals.

To such a one Miss Sarah Pierce, her preceptress at Litchfield Female Academy, wrote a moving farewell poem:

> May you my dear Mary, when delighted you roam
> Where the beams of the West, shed a bright genial ray
> Remember the friends, you have loved in your youth,
> Whose bosoms still glow, with affection and truth.

Dear Mary!—let us hope that, in spite of Miss Pierce's unusual punctuation, your own bosom glowed at this inspiriting valediction.

Schools for All

In a republic, ignorance is a crime.

—HORACE MANN

The subjects taught in the academies did not, as the rude old man suggested to his son, "go to Beelzebub." Rather the news of them spread like thin sunlight throughout the land, quickening seeds of interest. Knowledge, it now appeared, was not limited to Latin and religion. The academies, for all their lofty language and elegant manners, had introduced mathematics and the sciences to young America.

Such knowledge was needed. In this rapidly growing nation, farmers and builders, engineers and industrialists needed knowledge as much as clergymen and men of letters did. But so far, except for the handful of boys who had fought their way to an education, only the fortunate few could afford it.

And even the elementary schools were not living up to needs of the times. Swarms of people from other parts of the world were arriving in America to seek a new life, new opportunities to make a living from the land. Weary but hopeful they came. Most were peasants, accustomed only to working with the soil, dreaming of a few acres of their own. But too few were able to reach the open land. They were caught in cities and had to find whatever work they could. Towns were filled beyond the capacity of the "common" or free schools to take on their children. In Massachusetts, always the leading state in education, small children were working twelve hours a day in mills instead of learning how to read and write and live.

Meanwhile the district schools, cozy and homelike as they were, were often haphazard affairs, each at the mercy of its district's interest and funds. Some districts could boast a teacher who had been to an academy; others had only a youth or a young girl who managed to keep two steps ahead of the pupils. In many rural districts, school was kept open according to the state of the crops—that is, when the youngsters could be spared from the fields and the schoolmaster from his own farm labors.

In 1821, the first free high school was set up in Boston. Its stated purpose was to instruct the "sons of the mercantile and mechanic classes." To enter this school, a boy had to be twelve years old and know how to read, write, and figure simple sums. His courses, which went on for three years, were very like those of the academy: composition, grammar, declamation; mathematics, navigation, surveying; history, geography, and logic. Throughout these subjects, the boy was given heavy doses of those "philosophies" so dear to the academies, both moral and political. The young man who graduated, at the age of fourteen or fifteen, felt equipped to choose from several careers, from navigation to politics. Another high school soon opened in Worcester, Massachusetts; and New York, not to be outdone by the Yankees, started one in 1825. Indeed, Boston, always in the lead, even set up a high school for girls—with watered-down subjects, of course, as in the female academies. But the idea proved so popular and the number of girl applicants so large that the authorities gave up in despair and closed it down.

So in the first quarter of the nineteenth century the seeds of concern, planted by the academies, were sprouting. But they had a long, hard struggle before they bore much fruit. At the urging of James G. Carter, a farmer's son who graduated from Harvard, a law was passed in Massachusetts that required every town of five hundred families to provide free schools to teach, beyond the "three Rs," American history, algebra, geometry, surveying, and bookkeeping. Moreover, towns of more than four thousand inhabitants—cities, in those days—had to add general history, logic, rhetoric, Latin, and Greek to the curriculum. But the law was unpopular; the majority of the townspeople did not wish to be taxed for the education of other people's children. The law was altered, diluted, and largely ignored. Not until 1857 was it revived and made firm and strong.

Meanwhile a young man named Horace Mann was looking at the state of schools with interest and distress. Born of poor parents in 1796 in Franklin, Massachusetts, he had been a school-hungry boy himself. Until he was fifteen he had not had more than eight or ten weeks of schooling a year. But he was fortunate in that the pastor of the village church aided him with his studies; and at the age of nineteen he fell in with a good grammar-school (college preparatory) teacher who in six months helped him to enter the sophomore class of Brown University in Rhode Island, from which he graduated with highest honors. After teaching Latin and Greek for two years, he entered law school, was admitted to the bar, and before long became a state senator. In that position he was able to press for many reforms, none perhaps more important than the setting up of a state board of education to raise the standards of district and common schools.

"The schools at the present time," he said, "are so many independent communities, each being governed by its own habits, traditions and local customs. There is no common superintending power over them; there is no bond of brotherhood or family between them. They are strangers and alien to each other."

Horace Mann himself was made secretary of the new board. This meant that he had to resign from the state senate and embark on uphill work at a salary that never rose above thirty cents an hour—a poor wage, even in those days. But he succeeded in extracting two million dollars from the state for school buildings, new textbooks, and better salaries for teachers. Carter had tried to set up training schools for teachers; his law was defeated by a single vote. But now, with Mann in the saddle of the state board, teachers' schools were started in Massachusetts where would-be teachers could learn how best to cope with their young scholars. The first such school, in Lexington, consisted of one instructor and a student body of three girls! But the idea caught on, and schools and students grew in numbers. The course took only one year and was open to girls of sixteen and boys of seventeen. The training, in those early days, was not much more than a thorough going-over of elementary-school subjects, to be sure that the young teachers themselves could read and write and figure well enough to instruct the pupils. To show how low school standards of the time were, it must be added that many of the prospective teachers found this drill too difficult and dropped out before the end of the year!

Horace Mann was not yet content with what he had done for the children of Massachusetts. He sold his collection of law books to pay for a trip to Europe, where he spent some months studying foreign schools. From England, Holland, France, and particularly Germany, he brought back more ideas about how schools should be run. We remember how Pestalozzi had found new ways to make the job of learning interesting to children, encouraging them to use their own minds instead of merely commiting lines and rules to memory. "Papa" Pestalozzi's ideas, flouted at first by many people, had now taken hold in European countries, and Mann wrote about them in his famous Annual Reports to the people of Massachusetts.

The boys and girls of that state must have been particularly grateful for his recommendations on corporal punishment. In a typical school in that enlightened community, with an enrollment of four hundred pupils, the floggings averaged sixty-five a day. In Germany, Mann pointed out, flogging had long since been abolished, and he urged Massachusetts to follow suit. Many parents as well as schoolmen were horrified at the idea of controlling children without beating them, but Horace Mann was a persuasive fellow. As secretary of the board he had no authority to tell schools what they might or might not do. But his written reports had effect, and the teaching and discipline of youngsters in the state became more humane.

And as Massachusetts went, so, little by little, went the nation. Men of vision in other states cried out for state-supported free schools, secondary as well as elementary, for all young people. The call was answered, on many sides, by equally loud howls of horror. Free schools for the very poor?—yes; already there were paupers' schools in many cities. But free schools for everyone? why, that would mean a rise in taxes! Why should not able-bodied people pay for their own children's schooling?

"This bill will never pass!" shouted a Rhode Island legislator. "It's just as unreasonable to expect one man to give his money to educate another man's children as it is to expect one man to give his oxen to plow another man's corn!"

But the bill passed in Rhode Island—and in other states. Pennsylvania put up a fight, making free schools optional in the different districts, until as late as 1873. In that year the last school district gave in. No longer were any of the citizens of Pennsylvania required to declare themselves paupers before they could go to a free school.

And now the high school was flourishing. A lad could get a secondary education without paying academy fees or tramping for miles, like the Andover boy, in the hope that the school would allow him to work out his tuition. After the 1857 revival of the James G. Carter law, high schools sprang up like mushrooms throughout the state. Where in 1830 there had been 3 of them, by 1860 there were 102, with 200 more throughout the country. As late as 1874, however, a citizen of Kalamazoo sued the city for using his taxes for a high school for other people's children. But the Michigan supreme court ruled that this use of taxes was legal, and the Kalamazoo decision cemented the free high school into the law of the nation.

The heyday of the academies was over. Many of them were taken over by the towns, to become free, tax-supported schools under the new law. A number, such as Andover, still flourish as private schools of fine tradition and high standing. But with high schools opening their doors all over the country to boys and girls of whatever means, there was no actual need for private education.

The new high-school buildings were imposing—some of them, to our eyes, more like haunted castles than halls of learning; but they were designed in the most admired style of the day. Their courses, too, would seem musty and limited today. But compared to earlier curriculums, they offered a fine feast of knowledge. And they started a democratic trend in education that was to spread throughout the world.

Horace Mann, after serving twelve years on the Massachusetts school board, became president of Antioch, a coeducational college in Ohio, where he served until 1859. Looking around him and seeing what his efforts had accomplished for the lives of boys and girls, present and future, of his country, he must have felt the satisfaction of one who has worked hard for an ideal and sees it come true. In his last baccalaureate address at the college, he advised the graduating class: "Be ashamed to die until you have won some victory for humanity."

When he died a few weeks later, surely Horace Mann was not ashamed.

Epilogue

There is no doubt that the educational world is in a period of rapid transition. . . . The present is an age of experiment and investigation.

—Prof. F. V. N. PAINTER, 1886

These words were never more true than today. The "experiment" referred to was compulsory schooling beyond the elementary grades. For while more than three hundred public high schools had sprouted across the country, only seven states required young people to attend them. So new was the idea that all boys and girls should be put into school rather than tilling the soil or working in mills, that again there were outcries of "un-American!" "A threat to the rights of parents!" "School for everyone?—too costly for the taxpayer."

But one after another the states succumbed. Early in this century secondary schooling became the law of the land and Horace Mann's dream was realized. All young people were given an equal chance to learn, and under a single school system.

Today, more than fifty-one million young Americans flock in and out the doors of some 20,000 schools. While independent (private) schools abound, public schools provide free and equal schooling to children of all social classes, from kindergarten to university.

Considering their various beginnings, the schools of the world are surprisingly similar today. Chinese boys and girls now, too, have free and equal schooling. But Chinese students still spend a great deal of their school time learning to read and write because of the intricate symbols used in their language. There are some 40,000 of these word symbols, and even a lowly official must know at least 5,000 of them. Some attempts are now being made to introduce our Western alphabet into Chinese schools. Though strange, at first, to Oriental eyes, and not so beautiful as their brush-drawn characters, the phonetic alphabet may ease the burden of studies for future boys and girls of the Far East.

Russian schools stress patriotism, mathematics, and technology—a practical training toward building a new country. Free nursery schools welcome tots of two or three, thus freeing their mothers for work. Formal schooling begins at age seven. Dressed in uniforms, sitting straight as soldiers at their desks, the children study Russian and arithmetic, then go on to history, geography, and sciences.

In Europe, elementary schools are very like ours, though with longer hours and more homework. In recent years, however, the "modern" school has come into being. Like our comprehensive high school, it offers a groundwork in many subjects, both cultural and practical, and it is becoming increasingly popular.

But while the American school system has spread to other countries, our own schools, in turn, owe much to Europe. The ideas of the Swiss Pestalozzi, scoffed at by the early Yankees, have now long been embedded in our elementary schools. And the kindergarten, with its blocks and play and songs for young children, is so much a part of our school system that we tend to forget that it was once a startling idea from Germany, the brain child of young Friedrich Froebel. A Russian display at our centennial celebration in 1876 introduced the workshop and the use of tools into our schools. A few years later the Swedish *sloyd* program of arts and crafts was welcomed to American schoolrooms.

From Italy, early in this century, came the theories of Maria Montessori. While engaged in the patient training of backward children, Dr. Montessori, the first woman physician in Italy, cast her glance over the normal classrooms of Europe and was appalled. About children sitting stiffly in rows she wrote, "like butterflies transfixed by a pin." She set up her own school, the Casa dei Bambini, where the pupils were allowed to move about, and not only learned their letters and numbers from enticing playthings but eagerly dusted the furniture. Dr. Montessori's rules for feeding young children—bread soup, fried meatballs, and positively no raw vegetables—have mercifully been forgotten. But her love of children and her understanding of their capabilities live on in her theories of teaching.

More recently from England have come other school ideas. Summerhill, a small private coeducational boarding school, shocked the rest of the academic world by its free and easy ways. Similar private academies have since been set up in this country.

The newest idea from England, that of "open education," is gaining ground, particularly for young children. Here desks, grades, and formal lessons are done away with. The "open classroom," indeed, looks more like a playroom, with its low tables, plants, pets, books, paints, tools, and even a mattress on the floor for bouncing or napping.

The "age of experiment and investigation" is again upon us. The single school system, established in all good faith, is proving too rigid for today's needs. Parents and students balk at control by a remote board of education; therefore, decentralization has set in, giving communities a voice in running their schools.

What the schools of the future will be like no one can foretell. As societies and ways of living change, schools will change with them. Meanwhile, today's schools, however imperfect, have come a long way since those days when all knowledge was held in the minds of a few learned men who shared it with a few privileged students.

Bibliography

GENERAL

Atkinson, Carroll, and Maleska, Eugene T. *The Story of Education.* 2d ed. Philadelphia: Chilton, 1965.

Boyd, William. *The History of Western Education.* 8th ed. New York: Barnes & Noble, 1969.

Cole, Luella. *The History of Education: From Socrates to Montessori.* New York: Rinehart, 1950.

Cubberly, Ellwood P. *The History of Education.* Boston: Houghton, Mifflin, 1920.

—— *Readings in the History of Education.* Boston: Houghton, Mifflin, 1920.

Duggan, Stephen P. H. *A Student's Textbook in the History of Education.* New York: Appleton, 1948.

Good, Harry G., and Teller, James D. *History of Western Education.* 3d ed. New York: Macmillan, 1969.

Knight, Edgar Wallace. *Twenty Centuries of Education.* Boston and New York: Ginn, 1940.

McCormick, Patrick J. *History of Education.* Washington, D.C.: Catholic Educational Press, 1953.

Melvin, Arthur Gordon. *Education, a History.* New York: John Day, 1946.

Meyer, Adolphe E. *An Educational History of the Western World.* New York: McGraw-Hill, 1965.

Monroe, Paul. *A Brief Course in the History of Education.* New York: Macmillan, 1915.

BIBLIOGRAPHY

———— *Source-Book of the History of Education.* New York: Macmillan, 1910.

———— *A Textbook in the History of Education.* New York: Macmillan, 1905. Repr., New York: AMS Press, 1960.

————, ed. *A Cyclopedia of Education.* 5 vols. New York: Macmillan, 1928. Repr., Detroit: Gale, 1968.

Mulhern, James. *A History of Education.* 2d ed. New York: Ronald, 1946.

Painter, Franklin V. N. *A History of Education.* New York: Appleton, 1886. Repr. of 1904 rev. ed., St. Clair Shores, Mich.: Scholarly, 1970.

ANCIENT TIMES

Basham, Arthur L. *The Wonder That Was India: A Survey of the History and Culture of the Indian Sub-Continent before the Coming of the Muslims.* New York: Macmillan, 1954. Repr., New York: Grove, 1959.

Burland, Cottie A. *Ancient China.* Chester Springs, Pa.: Dufour, 1961.

Chiang Yee. *Chinese Calligraphy: An Introduction to Its Aesthetic and Technique.* London: Methuen, 1960.

Chiera, Edward. *They Wrote on Clay: The Babylonian Tablets Speak Today.* Chicago: University of Chicago Press, 1938.

Davidson, Thomas. *The Education of the Greek People and Its Influence on Civilization.* New York: Appleton, 1907. Repr., New York: AMS, [n.d.].

Eby, Frederick, and Arrowood, Charles F. *The History and Philosophy of Education, Ancient and Medieval.* New York: Prentice-Hall, 1940.

Graves, Frank Pierrepont. *A History of Education before the Middle Ages.* New York: Macmillan, 1925. Repr., New York: Gordon, [n.d.].

Marrou, Henri I. *A History of Education in Antiquity.* New York: Sheed & Ward, 1956. Repr., New York: New American Library, 1962.

Prodan, Mario. *Chinese Art.* New York: Pantheon, 1958.

Seeger, Elizabeth. *The Pageant of Chinese History.* 4th ed. New York: David McKay, 1962.

Smith, William A. *Ancient Education.* Westport, Conn.: Greenwood, 1955.

Southworth, Gertrude (Van Duyn), and Southworth, John Van Duyn. *Long Ago in the Old World: The Story of America's Old World Background from the Dawn of Civilization through the Period of Exploration.* Syracuse, N.Y.: Iroquois, 1959. (First pub-

Bibliography

lished in 1934 under the title: *America's Old World Background.*)

Woody, Thomas. *Life and Education in Early Societies.* New York: Macmillan, 1949. Repr., New York: Hafner, 1971.

MEDIEVAL TIMES

Alfric. *Colloquy.* Edited by George N. Garmonsway. New York: Appleton, 1966.

Graves, Frank Pierrepont. *History of Education during the Middle Ages.* New York: Macmillan, 1910. Repr., New York: Gordon, [n.d.].

Kirchner, Walther. *Western Civilization to 1500.* New York: Barnes & Noble, 1960.

Leach, Arthur Francis. *The Schools of Medieval England.* New York: Macmillan, 1915. Repr., New York: Blom, 1968.

Moncrieff, Ascott Robert Hope. *A Book about Schools, Schoolboys, Schoolmasters and Schoolbooks.* London: Black, 1925.

Origo, Iris. "The Education of Renaissance Man." *Horizon,* January 1960, pp. 57–68.

OLD ENGLAND

Clarke, Martin Lowther. *Classical Education in Britain, 1500–1900.* Cambridge: Cambridge University Press, 1959.

Curtis, Stanley J. *History of Education in Great Britain.* 3d ed. Westport, Conn.: Greenwood, 1971.

Dunlop, O. Jocelyn. *English Apprenticeship and Child Labour.* London: Unwin, 1912. Repr., Clifton, N.J.: Kelley, 1972.

Leach, Arthur Francis. *English Schools at the Reformation, 1546–1548.* London: Constable, 1896. Repr., New York: Russell, 1968.

Plimpton, George A. *The Education of Chaucer.* New York: Oxford, 1935. Repr., New York: AMS, [n.d.].

────── *The Education of Shakespeare.* New York: Oxford, 1933. Repr., Freeport, N.Y.: Books for Libraries, [n.d.].

Rodgers, John. *The Old Public Schools of England.* New York: Scribner's, 1938.

Stowe, A. R. Monroe. *English Grammar Schools in the Reign of Queen Elizabeth.* London: Constable, 1908.

Trevelyan, George M. *Illustrated English Social History.* 4 vols. New York: David McKay, 1942–52.

PESTALOZZIAN REFORMS

Guimps, Roger, Baron de. *Pestalozzi: His Life and Works.* New York: Appleton, 1890.

BIBLIOGRAPHY

Krüsi, Hermann. *Pestalozzi: His Life, Work and Influence.* New York: American Book Company, 1875.

Silber, Käte. *Pestalozzi: The Man and His Work.* London: Routledge & Kegan Paul, 1960.

Sleight, E. R. "Pestalozzi & the American Arithmetic." *National Mathematics Magazine,* Vol. XI, no 7, pp. 310–317 (Louisiana State U.).

UNITED STATES (EARLY)

Adams, James Truslow. *The Epic of America.* Boston: Little, Brown, 1931.

Beard, Charles A., and Beard, Mary R. *The Rise of American Civilization.* Rev. ed. New York: Macmillan, 1933.

Carpenter, Charles H. *A History of American Schoolbooks.* Philadelphia: University of Pennsylvania Press, 1963.

Feuss, Claude M. *An Old New England School: A History of Phillips Academy, Andover.* Boston: Houghton, Mifflin, 1917.

Givens, Willard Earl, and Farley, Belmont Mercer. *Our Public Schools.* Washington, D.C.: Supreme Council of Freemasonry, 1959.

Hall, Samuel Read. *Lectures on School-Keeping.* American Education: Its Men, Institutions and Ideas Series. Repr. of 1829 ed., New York: Arno, 1969.

Handlin, Oscar. *The Uprooted.* Boston: Little, Brown, 1951. Repr., New York: Grosset, 1971.

Johnson, Clifton. *Old Time Schools and School Books.* Repr. of 1904 ed., New York: Dover, 1963.

Littlefield, George E. *Early Schools and School-Books of New England.* Repr. of 1904 ed., New York: Russell, 1965.

Marr, Harriet Webster. *The Old New England Academies Founded before 1826.* New York: Comet, 1959.

Meyer, Adolphe E. *An Educational History of the American People.* 2d ed. New York: McGraw-Hill, 1967.

Middlekauff, Robert. *Ancients and Axioms: Secondary Education in Eighteenth-Century New England.* New Haven: Yale University Press, 1963. Repr., New York: Arno, 1972.

Moon, Glenn William, and MacGowan, John H. *Story of Our Land and People.* New York: Henry Holt, 1957.

Nietz, John Alfred. *Old Textbooks: Spelling, Grammar, Reading, Arithmetic, Geography, American History, Civil Government, Physiology, Penmanship, Art, Music, as Taught in the Common Schools from Colonial Days to 1900.* Pittsburgh: University of Pittsburgh Press, 1961.

Bibliography

Rudolph, Frederick, ed. *Essays on Education in the Early Republic.* Cambridge, Mass.: Harvard University Press, 1965.

Vanderpoel, Emily (Noyes), comp. *Chronicles of a Pioneer School from 1792 to 1833, Being the History of Miss Sarah Pierce and Her Litchfield School.* Edited by Elizabeth C. Barney Buel. Cambridge, Mass.: University Press, 1903.

MODERN TIMES

Cramer, John Francis, and Browne, George Stephenson. *Contemporary Education: A Comparative Study of National Systems.* 2d ed. New York: Harcourt, 1965.

Ellison, Martha. "Open Education, Not for the Tired or the Timid." *The Education Digest,* May 1972, pp. 8–11.

"Everything You Ever Wanted to Know about Open Education." *Teacher Magazine,* April 1972.

Goodman, Paul. *Compulsory Mis-Education.* New York: Vintage, 1964.

————— *New Reformation: Notes of a Neolithic Conservative.* New York: Vintage, 1971.

Greene, Mary Frances, and Ryan, Orletta. *The Schoolchildren: Growing Up in the Slums.* New York: Pantheon, 1966.

Grimsted, David Allen, and Grimsted, Patricia Kennedy. *Education in Changing Europe.* Sioux Falls: Sioux Falls Argus-Leader, 1962–63.

Hutchins, Robert M. *The Learning Society.* New York: Praeger, 1968.

Kerr, Anthony. *Schools of Europe.* Westminster, Md.: Canterbury, 1961.

Kogan, Maurice. *Informal Schools in Britain Today.* 2 vols. New York: Citation, 1972.

Kozol, Jonathan. *Free Schools.* Boston: Houghton, Mifflin, 1972.

Marcus, Sheldon, and Ravlin, Harry N., eds. *Conflicts in Urban Education.* New York: Basic, 1971.

Marin, Peter. "The Free School Nonmovement: Has Imagination Outstripped Reality?" *Saturday Review,* 22 July 1972, pp. 40–44.

Moehlman, Arthur Henry, and Roucek, Joseph S., eds. *Comparative Education.* New York: Dryden, 1951.

Montessori, Maria. *The Montessori Method.* New York: Macmillan, 1913. Rev. ed., New York: Schocken, 1964.

Neill, A. S. *Summerhill: A Radical Approach to Child Rearing.* New York: Hart, 1970.

New York City. Decentralization of the New York City Schools, Mayor's Advisory Panel on. *Reconnection for Learning: A Community School System for New York City.* New York: 1967.

BIBLIOGRAPHY

Nyquist, E., and Haus, Gene, eds. *Open Education: A Sourcebook for Parents and Teachers.* New York: Bantam, 1972.

Snitzer, Herb. *Summerhill, a Loving World.* New York: Macmillan, 1964.

——— *Summerhill: For and Against.* New York: Hart, 1970.

Ward, Florence Elizabeth. *The Montessori Method and the American School.* Repr. of 1913 ed., New York: Arno, 1971.

Wasserman, Miriam. *The School Fix, New York City, U.S.A.* New York: Simon & Schuster, 1971.

Weber, Lillian. *English Infant School and Informal Education.* Englewood Cliffs, N.J.: Prentice-Hall, 1971.

Wilbur, Donald Newton, ed. *The Nations of Asia.* New York: Hart, 1966.

Index

INDEX

Index